W9-AVC-940

Praise for *Secrets of a Good Life*

These quotes are smokin'!

—EMPEROR NERO

This may be the last quote book you'll ever need.

—SALOME

There's a whole lotta quotin' goin' on.

—ELVIS

A veritable Damascus Road experience!

—APOSTLE PAUL

Let them read quotes.

—MARIE ANTOINETTE

SECRETS
of A GOOD LIFE

AS TOLD *by* SAINTS
and SINNERS

COMPILED *and* INTRODUCED
by KATHLEEN STEPHENS

UPPER
ROOM BOOKS®
NASHVILLE

SECRETS OF A GOOD LIFE AS TOLD BY SAINTS AND SINNERS
Copyright © 2005 by Upper Room Books
All rights reserved.

No part of this book may be reproduced in any manner whatsoever without written permission of the publisher except in brief quotations embodied in critical articles or reviews. For information, write Upper Room Books, 1908 Grand Avenue, Nashville, TN 37212.

The Upper Room Web site: www.upperroom.org

Upper Room®, Upper Room Books®, and design logos are trademarks owned by Upper Room Ministries®, Nashville, Tennessee. All rights reserved.

At the time of publication all Web sites referenced in this book were valid. However, due to the fluid nature of the Internet, some addresses may have changed or the content may no longer be relevant.

Scripture quotations marked GNT are taken from the GOOD NEWS TRANSLATION, SECOND EDITION, © 1992 by American Bible Society. Used by permission. All rights reserved. Scripture quotations marked NEB are from The New English Bible © 1989 by Oxford University Press and Cambridge University Press. Reprinted by permission. Scripture quotations marked NIV are taken from the HOLY BIBLE, NEW INTERNATIONAL VERSION® (NIV)®. © 1973, 1978, 1984 by International Bible Society. Used by permission of Zondervan. All rights reserved. Scripture quotations marked NLT are taken from the *Holy Bible, New Living Translation,* © 1996. Used by permission of Tyndale House Publishers, Inc., Wheaton, Illinois 60189. All rights reserved. Scripture quotations marked NRSV are from the New Revised Standard Version of the Bible, © 1989, Division of Christian Education of the National Council of Churches of Christ in the United States of America. Used by permission. All rights reserved. Scripture quotations marked THE MESSAGE are from *The Message* by Eugene H. Peterson, © 1993, 1994, 1995, 1996, 2000, 2001, 2002. Used by permission of NavPress Publishing Group. All rights reserved.

Quotations from *Rock Stars on God* by Doug Van Pelt are © Relevant Media Group and are used with permission.
Quotations from Kyle Matthews (kylematthews.com) are used by permission. Credits begin on page 159 and constitute a continuation of this copyright page.

Cover design and interior icons: Wayne Brezinka / Brezinka Design Company
Cover Photo: © Thinkstock, courtesy of Gettyone.com
Interior design: Nancy Terzian / nterdesign.com
First printing: 2005

Library of Congress Cataloging-in-Publication Data
Secrets of a good life as told by saints and sinners / compiled and
introduced by Kathleen Stephens.
     p. cm.
  ISBN 0-8358-9811-3
  1. Christian life—Quotations, maxims, etc. I. Stephens, Kathleen.
  BV4501.3.S43 2005
  248.4—dc22   2005006070

Printed in the United States of America

C O N T E N T S

T H A N K S

Any quotation book first is indebted to those people whose wise words are recorded here. Gratitude also is due those who granted us permission to use the quotations; a complete list appears at the end of the book. Where possible, quotations were edited for inclusive language and consistency in style. Thanks also to Sarah Schaller-Linn and Denise Duke for suggesting many of the quotations and tracking full citations where possible. Several quotations in this book previously appeared as Daily Thoughtlets on www.Methodx.net, Upper Room Ministries' Web site for young adults.

Last, I'm grateful for the enthusiastic work of a team of twenty-somethings and friends whose vision made this book possible: Nicole Corlew, Bill Crenshaw, Jennifer Davis, Brandon Dyce, Rebecca Frame, Cary Graham, Debbie Gregory, Bill Lizor, Jane Massey, Sandy Miller, Heyda Negron-Perez, Tony Peterson, Robin Pippin, Beth Richardson, Ciona Rouse, Jeff Runyan, Soozung Sa, Lillian Smith, and Bill Treadway.

I N T R O D U C T I O N

Oh! Teach us to live well!
Teach us to live wisely and well!
—Psalm 90:12 (THE MESSAGE)

According to pop philosopher and former Beatle John Lennon, "Life is what happens to you while you're busy making other plans." Sometimes it seems we have little control over our lives. We can't predict how things will go for us or how long we will live. Only God knows.

But we can influence the real substance of our lives. We do that by choosing to live not *the* good life, which at least in Western culture means having lots of shiny stuff, but *a* good life. This life is marked by such character traits as "affection for others, exuberance about life, serenity, . . . willingness to stick with things, a sense of compassion in the heart, and a conviction that a basic holiness permeates things and people" (Galatians 5:22, THE MESSAGE). The Bible calls this living God's way.

Ultimately, having a good life means living in such a way that we can, at the end of our days, look back with no

9

regrets about the choices we have made. Before dismissing that lofty idea as unattainable, listen to the good news: Even if we've already made bad choices, all is not lost. For God-followers, every day can bring forgiveness and a fresh start. We can begin today applying wisdom to how we live the rest of our days.

The secrets of a good life can be found in all sorts of places. The obvious places to look are in holy scripture and in the writings of saints and other spiritual giants of all faiths. We also find wisdom for life in literature, poetry, music, film, and visual art. Sometimes the truest wisdom is found in the words of ordinary people—the "sinners" in the title of this book. Whether we find wisdom in the holy or the ordinary, our job is to recognize wisdom and eventually make it our own.

This book is full of wise quotations, arranged into seven secrets of a good life. Read the book straight through to discover all seven secrets, or dip into whatever section speaks to you at the moment.

Take time to read the quotations meditatively, mindfully, letting the truth sink into the deep places of your heart. That's how real transformation happens.

introduction

The quotations in this book comprise only a tiny fragment of the wisdom available to us. There is more to be found, even in the oddest places. The purpose of this book is to remind us of this truth:

Wisdom is everywhere.

Watch for it.

Acquire it.

Use it to live a good life.

introduction

PART 1

FIND YOUR PLACE

FIND YOUR PLACE

Living a good life first means finding our place in the world. Despite what we may have hoped, we are not the center of the universe! But neither are we insignificant nothings. Our place lies somewhere in between the two.

The Bible says, "Be honest in your estimate of yourselves" (Romans 12:3, NLT). That means seeing ourselves as creatures made in God's likeness, yet totally dependent on our Creator for the wisdom and energy needed to live a meaningful life.

Who hasn't wondered, *Why am I here? What am I supposed to do with my life? What did God have in mind for me when I was created?* Finding answers to those questions may take a lifetime of searching, but it's worth the effort. After all, as Euripides purportedly said, "There is just one life for each of us: our own."

14

From my perspective, good spiritual practice involves humility and compassion and ultimate forgiveness. And hopefully a degree of lightheartedness.

—MOBY

Do nothing from selfish ambition or conceit, but in humility regard others as better than yourselves.

—PHILIPPIANS 2:3 (NRSV)

Before his death, Rabbi Zusya said, "In the coming world, they will not ask me: 'Why were you not Moses?' They will ask me: 'Why were you not Zusya?'"

—MARTIN BUBER

No people have more occasion to be afraid of the approaches of pride than those who have made some advances in a pious life.   —WILLIAM LAW

Without poverty of spirit there can be no abundance of God.   —OSCAR ROMERO

find your place

Each time I get off a plane in Hollywood, I don't think
I'm pretty enough. —CHRISTINE LAHTI

Do not examine your gifts and options and find the best
combination that would yield a quality, economically
stable job. Examine your passions and pray and light
your candles. In many ways it doesn't matter what you
choose; what matters is how you are going to love.
—CHRISTOPHER DE VINCK

We should take care not to make the intellect our god;
it has, of course, powerful muscles, but no personality.
—ALBERT EINSTEIN

All people are frail, but you must admit that none is
more frail than yourself. —THOMAS À KEMPIS

Have patience with everything that remains unsolved in
your heart. Try to love the *questions themselves.*
—RAINER MARIA RILKE

A creature is not a creator, and cannot be. There is only one Creation, and we are its members.

—WENDELL BERRY

Man—a creature made at the end of the week's work when God was tired. —MARK TWAIN

Don't call me a saint—I don't want to be dismissed so easily. —DOROTHY DAY

Money, I never think of it. It always comes. The Lord sends it.

We do his work. He provides the means.

If he does not give us the means, that shows that he does not want the work. So why worry?

—MOTHER TERESA

If the soul is to know God, it must also forget itself and lose itself. For as long as it sees itself, it will not see and know God. —MEISTER ECKHARDT

I know what the great cure is: it is to give up, to relinquish, to surrender, so that our little hearts may beat in unison with the great heart of the world.

—HENRY MILLER

An adequate life . . . might be described as a life which has grasped intuitively the whole nature of things, and has seen and felt and refocused itself to this whole.

—DOUGLAS V. STEERE

From one ancestor [God] made all nations to inhabit the whole earth, and he allotted the times of their existence and the boundaries of the places where they would live, so that they would search for God and perhaps grope for him and find him—though indeed he is not far from each one of us.

—ACTS 17:26-27 (NRSV)

God created us for a purpose more astonishing and sublime than we can imagine.

—MARJORIE J. THOMPSON

Love is a servant even on the throne.

—PERCY C. AINSWORTH

The world is full of so-called prayer warriors who are prayer-ignorant. They're full of formulas and programs and advice, peddling techniques for getting what you want from God. Don't fall for that nonsense. This is your Father you are dealing with, and he knows better than you what you need. With a God like this loving you, you can pray very simply.

—JESUS, IN MATTHEW 6:7-8 (THE MESSAGE)

Ministers or priests and regular financial givers to the building fund are not the only ones who have callings. *All* Christians have a calling—the call to God. No circumstances of the job market or national economy can keep us from fulfilling that calling.

—GREGORY S. CLAPPER

Whatever I am, . . . O Lord, is laid bare before you.

—AUGUSTINE

find your place

To be humble in all our actions, to avoid every appearance of pride and vanity, to be meek and lowly in our words, actions, dress, behavior, and designs, in imitation of our blessed Savior, is to worship God in a higher manner than those who have only certain times to fall low on their knees in devotions.

—WILLIAM LAW

When pride comes, then comes disgrace; but wisdom is with the humble. —PROVERBS 11:2 (NRSV)

Use the things of this world as nature needs them, but not with excessive attachment. For it would be very displeasing to God if you were to set your heart on something of less value than yourself. That would be nothing but a surrender of your dignity.

—CATHERINE OF SIENA

Art is a collaboration between God and the artist, and the less the artist does, the better. —ANDRÉ GIDE

part 1

If you never commit yourself, you never express yourself, and yourself becomes less and less significant and decisive. Calculating selfishness is the annihilation of self.

—ANTON CHEKHOV

Proper timing is overrated. There's always a reason not to do things—it's too expensive, or it's not the best time, or this, or that—but I believe there are wonderful opportunities sailing by, and you have to be ready to grab them.

—MARY ENGELBREIT

Profound joy of the heart is like a magnet that indicates the path of life. One has to follow it, even though one enters into a way full of difficulties.

—MOTHER TERESA

The most secret, sacred wish that lies deep down at the bottom of your heart—the thing that you would rather die than have anyone else know of—that is just the very thing that God is wishing you to do or to be for him.

—EMMET FOX

find your place

The Spirit of love says: "Don't be afraid to let go of your need to control your own life. Let me fulfill the true desire of your heart."   —HENRI J. M. NOUWEN

We are not here to show something to God. We are here because God—the One who wants to be completely known—has something to show to us.

—ROBERT BENSON

Don't ask yourself what the world needs. Ask yourself what makes you come alive, and go do that, because what the world needs is people who have come alive.

—HOWARD THURMAN

I believe that God made me for a purpose. . . . But he also made me fast. And when I run, I feel his pleasure.

—ERIC LIDDELL, IN *CHARIOTS OF FIRE* (FILM, 1981)

God's loving voice calls your name and then says, "Let there be *you*."   —FLORA SLOSSON WUELLNER

There can be nothing so reasonable and pious as to have no will but God's and to desire nothing for ourselves in our persons, our state, and condition but what the good providence of God appoints for us.

—WILLIAM LAW

Think of yourself as incandescent power, illuminated perhaps and forever talked to by God and his messengers.

—BRENDA UELAND

Do not wait for leaders; do it alone, person to person.

—MOTHER TERESA

It's not my wish to admire the mystics, but to let them re-collect me so that daily I see the inner light as clearly as possible, for it is hidden also within me.

—DOROTHEE SOELLE

Even if you're on the right track, you'll get run over if you just sit there.

—WILL ROGERS

find your place

It's one of life's great mysteries, isn't it? Why are we here? I mean, are we the product of some cosmic coincidence? Or is there a God, you know, watching everything, with a plan for us and stuff? I don't know, man, but it keeps me up at night.

—GRIF, IN *RED VS. BLUE* (VIDEO, 2003)

Let me tell you why you are here. You're here to be salt-seasoning that brings out the God-flavors of this earth. If you lose your saltiness, how will people taste godliness? . . .

Here's another way to put it: You're here to be light, bringing out the God-colors in the world. God is not a secret to be kept.

—JESUS, IN MATTHEW 5:13-14 (THE MESSAGE)

Man is born to live, not to prepare for life.

—BORIS PASTERNAK

Nothing in life is accidental. He who believes in accident does not believe in God.   —ALEXANDER YELCHANINOV

Jesus came into the world as light to brighten every dark corner. To follow him means to reflect his truth. The world waits. Shine like a light!

—JOYCE HOLLYDAY

Our work is . . . a joyful response of thanksgiving and gratitude for all God has done and all God is. . . . We *must* ask if the life we are living is a worthy expression of gratitude for what God has done for us.

—GREGORY S. CLAPPER

Don't be wishing you were someplace else or with someone else. Where you are right now is God's place for you. Live and obey and love and believe right there. God, not your marital status, defines your life.

—1 CORINTHIANS 7:17 (THE MESSAGE)

You didn't choose me, remember; I chose you, and put you in the world to bear fruit, fruit that won't spoil.

—JESUS, IN JOHN 15:16 (THE MESSAGE)

Jesus gave us a new norm of greatness. If you want to be important—wonderful. If you want to be recognized—wonderful. If you want to be great—wonderful. But recognize that he who is greatest among you shall be your servant. That's your new definition of greatness.

—MARTIN LUTHER KING JR.

God never requires anything of his creations that he didn't already build into them.

—MYLES MUNROE

God does not lead us all by the same road.

—TERESA OF AVILA

Life is a great big canvas, and you should throw all the paint on it you can.   —DANNY KAYE

When we see that each life is ennobled by the call of God and made fruitful by Christ's risen life, we are able to take each day as it comes, as a fresh gift from God.

—OLIVE WYON

Schools teach you to imitate. . . . you were supposed to imitate the teacher in such a way as to convince the teacher you were not imitating. . . . That got you A's. Originality, on the other hand, could get you anything— from A to F. —ROBERT M. PIRSIG

We are as sure that nothing happens to us by chance as that the world itself was not made by chance. We are as certain that all things happen and work together for our good as that God is goodness itself.

—WILLIAM LAW

We might have much peace if we were not such busy-bodies, for what others say and do is no concern of ours.

—THOMAS À KEMPIS

Each morning is a new beginning of our life. Each day is a finished whole. The present day marks the boundary of our cares and concerns. It is long enough to find God or to lose him, to keep faith or fall into disgrace.

—DIETRICH BONHOEFFER

find your place

We are disabused of original giftedness in the first half of our lives. Then—if we are awake, aware, and able to admit our loss—we spend the second half trying to recover and reclaim the gift we once possessed.

—PARKER J. PALMER

Daring to dream what is deepest in our collective longings is what makes us most human and fully alive.

—WENDY M. WRIGHT

When I look at the galaxies on a clear night—when I look at the incredible brilliance of creation, and think that this is what God is like, then, instead of feeling intimidated and diminished by it, I am enlarged—I rejoice that I am part of it.   —MADELEINE L'ENGLE

I doubt if we nuns are really as self-sacrificing as we must seem to be to you who live in the world. We don't give everything for nothing, you know. The Mystery plays fair.   —ELIZABETH GOUDGE

Faith alone can give us the light to see that God's will is to be found in our everyday life. Without this light, we cannot see to make the right decisions. Without this certitude we cannot have supernatural confidence and peace. We stumble and fall constantly even when we are most enlightened. —THOMAS MERTON

Our challenge is to have faith—in failure, in success, in whatever life brings. The unexpected turns, the painful endings, the precarious beginnings are all part of the path of faith, where we are reminded with each step that the Resurrection did not happen only once long ago, it happens each day of our lives.

—JEAN M. BLOMQUIST

Do what you love; the money will follow.

—MARSHA SINETAR

The meaning of our existence is not invented by ourselves, but rather detected. —VIKTOR FRANKL

find your place

I would invite you to consider your calling. . . . Don't just go where you're directed or even invited, but rather where your own moral compass leads you. And don't accept others' notions of what is possible or realistic; dare to dream things and don't be afraid to take risks.

—JIM WALLIS

You have an obligation to have an extraordinary life.

—CHRISTOPHER DE VINCK

The surest way into the heart of God is to be still. In being still we learn to be attentive to the vast and hidden stillness that permeates all things.

—WENDY M. WRIGHT

Vocation does not come from willfulness. It comes from listening. I must listen to my life and try to understand what it is truly about—quite apart from what I would like it to be about—or my life will never represent anything real in the world, no matter how earnest my intentions.

—PARKER J. PALMER

God created day and night for us so we need not wander without boundaries, but may be able to see every morning the goal of the evening ahead.

—DIETRICH BONHOEFFER

If you care about something, you have to protect it—if you're lucky enough to find a way of life you love, you have to find the courage to *live* it.

—JOHN IRVING

The answer does not lie in having to embrace Judaism, Buddhism, fundamentalism, Catholicism, or any other *ism.* Nor does it lie in mere belief in God. Believing is of limited use. Sacred scriptures and inspired writings can point the way, but finally you have to walk where they are pointing. This you can do with the aid of a system or by listening to the stillness within you. Either way is fine, but ultimately you must stop searching and simply do it.

—HUGH PRATHER

find your place

PART 2

CONNECT WITH THE SOURCE

CONNECT WITH THE SOURCE

Is it possible to know God, the Source of all things? The idea may seem outlandish—until with a heart full of faith we ourselves connect with God. And that connection with God—spirit to Spirit—makes all the difference between living a good life and a ho-hum life.

Connecting with God transforms us, giving our lives meaning, purpose, and a peace that comes from believing that God is both strong and loving. As religious scholar J. I. Packer wrote, "Once you become aware that the main business that you are here for is to know God, most of life's problems fall into place of their own accord."

34

The people I've met who reject Christianity tend to be mostly against what they know of Christians, not Jesus himself. In fact, most of them are actually quite open to the person of Jesus. They sense no pretense, no ulterior motive. He simply says, "Come to me." . . . He knows that while we tend to resist arm-twisting and resent being lectured to, we seldom doubt our own experience.

—KYLE MATTHEWS

It is easier to gaze into the sun than into the face of the mystery of God. Such is its beauty and its radiance.

—HILDEGARD OF BINGEN

We cannot take a step toward the heavens. God crosses the universe and comes to us.

—SIMONE WEIL

Good is relevant. Beauty's relevant. Everything's relevant. Except for me. I'm absolute.

—GOD, IN *JOAN OF ARCADIA*
(TELEVISION SHOW, 2003)

connect with the source

Worship no god but me.   —GOD, IN EXODUS 20:3 (GNT)

In prayer there is a connection between what God does and what you do. You can't get forgiveness from God, for instance, without also forgiving others. If you refuse to do your part, you cut yourself off from God's part.
                    —JESUS, IN MATTHEW 6:14-15 (THE MESSAGE)

Every day people are straying away from the church and going back to God.   —LENNY BRUCE

How much did I hear of religion as a child? Very little, and yet my heart leaped when I heard the name of God. I do believe every soul has a tendency toward God.
                                        —DOROTHY DAY

I'm afraid that God is speaking and no one is listening.
                    —DANA SCULLY, IN THE X FILES
                        (TELEVISION SHOW, 1993)

Have a habitual desire to imitate Christ in all your deeds by bringing your life into conformity with his. You must then study his life in order to know how to imitate him and behave in all events as he would.

—JOHN OF THE CROSS

Human beings have neither the aural nor the psychological capacity to withstand the awesome power of God's true voice. Were you to hear it, your mind would cave in and your heart would explode within your chest. We went through five Adams before we figured that out.   —METATRON, IN *DOGMA* (FILM, 1999)

Deep within us all there is an amazing inner sanctuary of the soul, a holy place, a Divine Center, a speaking Voice, to which we may continually return. Eternity is at our hearts, pressing upon our time-torn lives, warming us with intimations of an astounding destiny, calling us home unto Itself.   —THOMAS R. KELLY

Starting from scratch, [God] made the entire human race and made the earth hospitable, with plenty of time and space for living so we could seek after God, and not just grope around in the dark but actually *find* him. He doesn't play hide-and-seek with us. He's not remote; he's *near*. —ACTS 17:26-27 (THE MESSAGE)

I love those who love me, and those who seek me diligently find me. —GOD, IN PROVERBS 8:17 (NRSV)

Your Beloved will not share you with others—that is his nature; he wants to be first in your heart, as you are in his. If you knew how to disentangle from your own confused feelings, Jesus would gladly stay with you.

—THOMAS À KEMPIS

Here's what I don't get about you: You know for a fact that there is a God. You have been in his presence. He's spoken to you personally, and yet I just heard you claim to be an atheist.

—BARTLEBY, IN *DOGMA* (FILM, 1999)

God, I like you so much better with some distance between us.

—EDDIE, IN *KEEN EDDIE* (TELEVISION SHOW, 2003)

O Lord, . . . you have formed us for yourself, and our hearts are restless till they find rest in you.

—AUGUSTINE

Jesus . . . was a free spirit who had a lovely wildness in him. Every time religious institutions . . . tried to box him in, he danced away from their threats and trick questions effortlessly. It is enthralling that there are twenty-six or twenty-seven years of his life about which we know nothing. —JOHN O'DONOHUE

You and I are called to nothing less than participation in the life of God. . . . Everything that happens to us, everyone we meet can be a gateway to God if we are open and listening for his message coming in and through them. —EILEEN LYDDON

connect with the source

As actions are of much more significance than words, it must be a much more acceptable worship to glorify God in all the actions of our common life than with any little form of words at any particular times.

—WILLIAM LAW

O Fairness, so ancient, and yet so new! I loved you too late.
—AUGUSTINE

Union with God is neither acquired nor received; it is *realized*, and in that sense it is something that can be yearned for, sought after, and—with God's grace—found.
—GERALD G. MAY

The most important thing that I know is dependence on Christ. That's all I know.
—ALICE COOPER

Jesus is honey in the mouth, music in the ear, and a shout of joy in the heart.

—BERNARD OF CLAIRVAUX

part 2

If any of you is lacking in wisdom, ask God, who gives to all generously and ungrudgingly, and it will be given you. But ask in faith, never doubting, for the one who doubts is like a wave of the sea, driven and tossed by the wind. —JAMES 1:5-6 (NRSV)

Read your Bibles, but *that isn't being religious.* Read your Bibles, and feel your way back into that Source and Spring of Life which bubbled up in the Bible-writers. And you'll find that Source and Spring of Life bubbling up *within you also.* —THOMAS R. KELLY

Indeed God is mysterious. . . . In the end, it is not this mystery that keeps us from God. The mystery is in fact part of what draws us to God.

—GREGORY S. CLAPPER

How do you know God's a he? He can be a she. You don't know that. —SHALIKA, IN *BOYZ N THE HOOD* (FILM, 1991)

connect with the source

As long as it is real, as long as we hide nothing from God of what we are really feeling—anger and joy, frustration and thanksgiving—our prayer is good.

—SUSAN MUTO

God is always bigger than the boxes we build for God, so we should not waste too much time protecting the boxes.

—RICHARD ROHR

We are transfigured much like the Messiah, our lives gradually becoming brighter and more beautiful as God enters our lives and we become like him.

—2 CORINTHIANS 3:18 (THE MESSAGE)

I think that God in creating man somewhat overestimated his ability.

—OSCAR WILDE

Teach me to do your will, for you are my God. Let your good spirit lead me on a level path.

—PSALM 143:10 (NRSV)

part 2

As a deer longs for flowing streams, so my soul longs for you, O God. —PSALM 42:1 (NRSV)

In the evening I went very unwillingly to a society in Aldersgate Street, where one was reading Luther's Preface to the Epistle to the Romans. About a quarter before nine, while he was describing the change which God works in the heart through faith in Christ, I felt my heart strangely warmed. I felt I did trust in Christ, Christ alone for salvation, and an assurance was given me that he had taken away *my* sins, even *mine,* and saved *me* from the law of sin and death.

—JOHN WESLEY

Sometimes I like to sound old-timey.

—GOD, IN *JOAN OF ARCADIA*
(TELEVISION SHOW, 2003)

I spat at God once. Never again.

—TSAR NICHOLAS II, IN *RASPUTIN*
(FILM, 1996)

connect with the source

As bees can never remain upon anything decayed but only among flowers, so also our heart finds rest solely in God, and no creature can ever satisfy it.

—Francis de Sales

Did you think that because he's such a nice God, he'd let you off the hook? Better think this one through from the beginning. God is kind, but he's not soft. In kindness he takes us firmly by the hand and leads us into a radical life change.

—Romans 2:4 (The Message)

Nobody talks so constantly about God as those who insist that there is no God.

—Heywood Broun

Christ comforts and heals, saves and forgives . . .; but we must not forget that he judges too. If we truly love him, we will love *everything* in him; not only his compassion and mercy, but his sharpness too. It is his sharpness that prunes and purifies.

—J. Heinrich Arnold

part 2

How powerful is a pure love of Jesus, untainted by self-interest or self-love! —THOMAS À KEMPIS

God gives us many gifts, but never permanence; that we must seek in his arms. —SHELDON VANAUKEN

God is God of all—those we love and those we do not love. —RON DELBENE

God is clever, but not dishonest. —ALBERT EINSTEIN

The one great sin for us human beings is to live in the darkness of our own isolated loneliness. We were made for a loving union with God and all human beings. —GEORGE A. MALONEY

We cannot love God if we do not know God. —N. GRAHAM STANDISH

connect with the source

Your friendship with God is rooted in a paradox.
You reach to God as you seek to maintain a critical
balance—the balance between intimacy and awe.

—CALVIN MILLER

As Christ comes into us, other people will be drawn to
us because he is literally the most attractive Being in
the universe. —W. E. SANGSTER

Blessed be God forever for all his bounties! Amen.

—BRIGITTA OF SWEDEN

Christ is born into our hearts' stillness, not just today
but every moment. He is the turning point of all our
nights. Be still and know that he is God.

—MARGARET SILF

God don't make no mistakes; that's how he got to be God.

—ARCHIE BUNKER, IN *ALL IN THE FAMILY*
(TELEVISION SHOW, 1971)

part 2

Yes, I rather like this God fellow. He's very theatrical, you know: a pestilence here, a plague there. Omnipotence—gotta get me some of that.

—STEWIE GRIFFIN, IN *FAMILY GUY*
(TELEVISION SHOW, 1999)

Wherever we open our eyes
or our ears catch the murmur of creation,
God is speaking to us.   —OSCAR ROMERO

From this moment on, dearest Lord, there is nothing which I am not prepared to undertake for love of you.

—COLETTE

Let us do what Our Lord did and rise early in the morning, [while] everything is at rest in silence and darkness. . . . Let us rise and watch with God, lifting our hearts to him, laying our souls at his feet, and at this early hour when [prayer] is so secret and so sweet, let us fall at his feet and enjoy [conversation] with Our Creator.

—CHARLES DE FOUCAULD

connect with the source

Just as the sun cannot stop shining, so God cannot stop loving. And the whole history of mankind is the history of man's struggle to learn how to perceive and return the Love that God bestows . . . so freely.

—Toyohiko Kagawa

Most of us cannot or will not embrace the monastic life. . . . But we can attend to the question of a rule of life. What might that mean for each of us? How might we create windows and gateways in our daily lives?

—Wendy M. Wright

All that a Christian does, even in eating and sleeping, is prayer, when it is done in simplicity, according to the order of God, without either adding to or diminishing from it by his own choice.

—John Wesley

Doubts and questions . . . signal a healthy faith. You're not in trouble when you doubt. You're only in trouble when you stop caring.

—Thomas Ettinger and Helen Neinast

Prayer moves from knowing about God to knowing
God.   —MARIA BOULDING

When I put Christ, and Christ's love, at the centre, then
that means that I say "Yes" to recognizing that love and
letting myself receive that love, standing under that
great outpouring of love as I might stand in the midst
of a shower of rain or a burst of sunlight.

—ESTHER DE WAAL

We were never meant to try to *imitate* Christ, any more
than a fish imitates the water or a bird imitates the air.
We are to *abide* in the Christ.

—FLORA SLOSSON WUELLNER

49

Prayer comes only as a gift; what we do is ready
ourselves for the gift. All the techniques we read about
are really ways of bringing ourselves to that stillness
where the voice of God can be heard.

—KATHLEEN FISCHER

Every morning God gives us the gift of comprehending anew his faithfulness of old; thus, in the midst of our life with God, we may daily begin a new life with him.

—DIETRICH BONHOEFFER

Your creation sings praise to you so that we may love you, and we love you so that praise may be offered to you by your creation.

—AUGUSTINE

God is always coming because he is life, and life has the unbridled force of creation.

God comes because he is light, and light may not remain hidden.

God comes because he is love, and love needs to give of itself. God has always been coming; God is always coming.

—CARLO CARRETTO

Faith gives wings to prayer, and without it no one can fly upward to heaven.

—JOHN CLIMACUS

part 2

In the maddening maze of things,
And tossed by storm and flood,
To one fixed trust my spirit clings;
I know that God is good!

—JOHN GREENLEAF WHITTIER

As a very little dust will disorder a clock, and the least
sand will obscure our sight, so the least grain of sin
which is upon the heart will hinder its right motion
towards God. —JOHN WESLEY

God has always been to me not so much like a father as
like a dear and tender mother.

—HARRIET BEECHER STOWE

Knowing God is to enter into a whole way of life. It is
being caught up into a liberating, tender love on the
part of the omnipotent God, made manifest as a spoken
Word in his Son, Jesus Christ.

—GEORGE A. MALONEY

connect with the source

Unless we are to remain befogged and bewildered and give up all hope of ever knowing God as a Person, we have to accept his own planned focusing of himself in a human being, Jesus Christ. —J. B. PHILLIPS

Our real selves are all waiting for us in [God]. It is no good trying to "be myself" without him. The more I resist him and try to live on my own, the more I become dominated by my own heredity and upbringing and surroundings and natural desires.

—C. S. LEWIS

I adore Thee, O my God, as the true and only Light! —JOHN HENRY NEWMAN

Holiness is not the fruit of specialness, but of faithfulness. For to be faithful in a relationship is to honor it by the way we live. The call to holiness in our day, as it has always been, is a call to live in the world as a sign of the Kingdom. —JAMES C. FENHAGEN

The true secret of making contact with God is littleness, simplicity of heart, poverty of spirit: all the things that pride, wealth, and cleverness foil in us.

—CARLO CARRETTO

Until I am essentially united with God, I can never have full rest or real happiness. —JULIAN OF NORWICH

It is the will to pray that is the essence of prayer, and the desire to find God, to see him, and to love him is the one thing that matters.

—THOMAS MERTON

Prayer is a hunger, a hunger that is not easily quieted.

—EDWARD FARRELL

Sophia wished that Florence would not talk about the Almighty as if his real name was Godfrey, and God was just Florence's nickname for him.

—NANCY MITFORD

connect with the source

God is not a cosmic bellboy for whom we can press a
button to get things.   —HARRY EMERSON FOSDICK

Me and God—we'd be mates!
                        —MICHAEL J. "CROCODILE" DUNDEE,
                        IN *CROCODILE DUNDEE* (FILM, 1986)

The art of praying . . . is really the art of learning to
waste time gracefully—to be simply the clay in the
hands of the potter. This may sound easy—too easy to
be true—but it is really the most difficult thing we ever
learn to do.   —THOMAS H. GREEN

Oddly enough, the only place to find God in the middle
of all the noise and pressure is just that—in the middle
of all the noise and pressure.
                —THOMAS C. ETTINGER AND HELEN R. NEINAST

Thank God, I am still an atheist.

                                        —LUIS BUÑUEL

PART 3

BELONG TO A VILLAGE

BELONG TO A VILLAGE

We all need human companionship. In fact, we were made for it. Loving and being loved makes us feel alive and puts an extra spring in our step. When we know we're loved, we feel at home no matter how far from home we are.

But cultivating community can be dicey. It takes a lot of work and is often messy. As C. S. Lewis wrote, "Love anything, and your heart will certainly be wrung and possibly be broken."

Yet despite the risks, we want to belong to a village, a welcoming community of folks who care about us. Without community, life doesn't seem worth the effort. With it, we can take all that life throws at us and keep standing, all the while thinking of the stories we're going to tell when we get back home.

Call it a clan, call it a network, call it a tribe, call it a family. Whatever you call it, whoever you are, you need one.   —JANE HOWARD

Having someone wonder where you are when you don't come home at night is a very old human need.

—MARGARET MEAD

The love of our neighbor in all its fullness simply means being able to say to him: "What are you going through?"

—SIMONE WEIL

God arranged the members in the body, each one of them, as he chose. If all were a single member, where would the body be?

—I CORINTHIANS 12:18-19 (NRSV)

Community begins to form when each person tries to welcome and love the others as they are.

—JEAN VANIER

belong to a village

Friendship is only true in those you bind together, joined to you by your love poured into our hearts through the Holy Spirit that has been given to us.

—AUGUSTINE

There is nothing that makes us love a person so much as praying for him or her. . . . By considering yourself an advocate with God for your neighbors and friends, you would never find it hard to be at peace with them.

—WILLIAM LAW

Two are better than one, because they have a good reward for their toil. For if they fall, one will lift up the other; but woe to one who is alone and falls and does not have another to help.

—ECCLESIASTES 4:9-10 (NRSV)

If we hate ourselves, we can never love others, for love is the gift of oneself. How will you make a gift of that which you hate? —WILLIAM SLOANE COFFIN

Love is had only by loving. If you want love, you must begin by loving—I mean you must want to love. Once you want it, you must open the eye of your understanding to see where and how love is to be found, and you will find it within your very self.

—Catherine of Siena

God is making room in my heart for compassion: the awareness that where my life begins is where your life begins.

—Howard Thurman

What is hell? . . . The suffering of being no longer able to love.

—Fyodor Dostoyevsky

How wonderful it is, how pleasant, for God's people to live together in harmony!

—Psalm 133:1 (GNT)

Family life! The United Nations is child's play compared to the tugs and splits and need to understand and forgive in any family.

—May Sarton

belong to a village

Another plan I have is World Peace through Formal
Introductions. . . . My theory is, if you knew everyone
in the world personally, you'd be less inclined to fight
them in a war: "Who? The Malaysians? Are you kidding?
I know those people!" —GEORGE CARLIN

Ah, how much I like you, how well we get on, when
you're asleep and I'm awake. —COLETTE

Within our family there was no such thing as a person who
did not matter. Second cousins thrice removed mattered.
We knew—and thriftily made use of—everybody's
middle name. We knew who was buried where. We all
mattered, and the dead most of all.

—SHIRLEY ABBOTT

A family can be made up of any combination of people,
heterosexual or homosexual, who share their lives in an
intimate (not necessarily sexual) way. . . . Wherever
there is lasting love, there is a family.

—SHERE HITE

You have enemies, for who can live on this earth
without them? For your own sake, love them. In no
way can your enemies so hurt you by their violence as
you hurt yourself if you do not love them.

—Augustine

Many people are looking for an ear that will listen.
They do not find it among Christians, because these
Christians are talking where they should be listening.

—Dietrich Bonhoeffer

God's best microphone is Christ,
and Christ's best microphone is the church,
and the church is all of you.

—Oscar Romero

Those of us who are strong and able in the faith need
to step in and lend a hand to those who falter, and not
just do what is most convenient for us. Strength is for
service, not status.   —Romans 15:1 (The Message)

belong to a village

The important thing is not to think much but to love much; do, then, whatever most arouses you to love.

—TERESA OF AVILA

We must either love or hate, and not to love is to hate. . . . Let us not forget this tremendous danger in which we exist. To forget is to have made your choice.

—SØREN KIERKEGAARD

Love your neighbor as you love yourself.

—JESUS, IN MATTHEW 22:39 (GNT)

True friends are those who really know you but love you anyway.

—EDNA BUCHANAN

In so far as we carry through life a cheerful, patient, responsive, and unselfish spirit, we shall be doing something every day to make the burden of others easier to be borne.

—PERCY C. AINSWORTH

It's the ones you can call up at 4:00 AM that matter.

—MARLENE DIETRICH

Friends are the family we choose for ourselves.

—EDNA BUCHANAN

There is a new wave of people who crave real relationship and are willing to sacrifice technology for experience.

—PENNY FORD

Many people believe that the opposite of love is hate, but that's not true. The opposite of love is apathy.

—HELEN R. NEINAST AND THOMAS C. ETTINGER

Let him who cannot be alone beware of community. Let him who is not in community beware of being alone.

—DIETRICH BONHOEFFER

Hospitality is made up of hard work undertaken under risky conditions.

—ANA MARÍA PINEDA

belong to a village

Our own sense of belonging is found not by excluding others but by including them.

—Marilyn Brown Oden

It is a great advantage for us to be able to consult someone who knows us, so that we may learn to know ourselves.   —Teresa of Avila

I give you a new commandment, that you love one another. Just as I have loved you, you also should love one another.   —Jesus, in John 13:34 (nrsv)

Effective companionship begins with a willingness to sit still long enough to listen and let insight emerge.

—Timothy Jones

Tell me who your friends are, and I will tell you what you stand for. Our spirits are etched by those among whom we live and work. We become like those to whom we give ourselves.   —Joan Puls

I want to have boundless charity, especially toward those who do not attract me.

—ELIZABETH LESEUR

Love from the center of who you are; don't fake it.

—ROMANS 12:9 (THE MESSAGE)

Welcome with open arms fellow believers who don't see things the way you do. And don't jump all over them every time they do or say something you don't agree with . . . . Remember, they have their own history to deal with. Treat them gently.

—ROMANS 14:1 (THE MESSAGE)

When we honestly ask ourselves which persons in our lives mean the most to us, we often find that it is those who, instead of giving much advice, solutions, or cures, have chosen rather to share our pain and touch our wounds with a gentle and tender hand.

—HENRI J. M. NOUWEN

belong to a village

The mystery of the poor is this: that they are Jesus, and what you do for them you do for him. It is the only way we have of knowing and believing in our love.

—DOROTHY DAY

Great healing and insight can come simply by spending time in the presence of someone who hears us out.

—TIMOTHY JONES

As far as I am concerned, the greatest suffering is to feel alone, unwanted, unloved.

—MOTHER TERESA

66

Piglet sidled up to Pooh from behind. "Pooh!" he whispered. "Yes, Piglet?" "Nothing," said Piglet, taking Pooh's paw. "I just wanted to be sure of you."

—A. A. MILNE

You can learn a lot from hanging out with people with gray hair.

—DOUG VAN PELT

The whole congregation of believers was united as one—one heart, one mind! They didn't even claim ownership of their own possessions. No one said, "That's mine; you can't have it." They shared everything.

—Acts 4:32 (The Message)

If there are poor on the moon, we will go there too.

—Mother Teresa

Secret prayer for others all during the day is an acid test of our unselfishness. Our little selves must fade out, leaving a self-forgetting channel, through which God's warmth flows unhindered in lovely unending prayer.

—Frank C. Laubach

The only way I can prove my love is by scattering flowers, and these flowers are every little sacrifice, every glance and word, and the doing of the least of actions for love.

—Thérèse of Lisieux

belong to a village

The price of shallow sex may be a corresponding loss of capacity for deep love. —SHANA ALEXANDER

Our society is filled with people for whom the sexual relationship is one where body meets body but where person fails to meet person.

—FREDERICK BUECHNER

Sex without a commitment, no matter how many "I love you's" you say or hear, is really only about what you can get, because you are essentially saying, "I know this could hurt both of us, but my needs right now are more important than your potential pain."

—SHELLIE R. WARREN

Sex is hardly ever just about sex.

—SHIRLEY MacLAINE

Sex divorced from love is the thief of personal dignity.

—CAITLIN THOMAS

68

A spiritual friend is someone with whom it is safe to take apart our shallow faith, our compulsive addictions, or whatever else might be under the surface of our visible lives. He or she will help us to exchange our weaknesses for a new source of trust, conviction, and desire.

—JAMES HOUSTON

Love anything, and your heart will certainly be wrung and possibly be broken. If you want to make sure of keeping it intact, . . . lock it up safe in the casket or coffin of your selfishness. But in that casket . . . it will change. . . ; it will become unbreakable, impenetrable, irredeemable.

—C. S. LEWIS

The longer we journey on the road to unity, the more the sense of belonging grows and deepens. The sense is not just one of belonging to a community. It is a sense of belonging to the universe, to the earth, to the air, to the water, to everything that lives, to all humanity.

—JEAN VANIER

Every existing thing is equally upheld in its existence by God's creative love. The friends of God should love him to the point of merging their love into his with regard to all things here below. —SIMONE WEIL

You *must* get along with each other. You must learn to be considerate of one another, cultivating a life in common. —1 CORINTHIANS 1:10 (THE MESSAGE)

Our one aim must be to try to put love and humility first in our prayers and our desires, to be resolved never to let indifference or impatience or irritation or evasion take the place of the will to love.

—OLIVE WYON

In Christ's family there can be no division into Jew and non-Jew, slave and free, male and female. Among us you are all equal. That is, we are all in a common relationship with Jesus Christ.

—GALATIANS 3:28 (THE MESSAGE)

The heaven of heavens is love. There is nothing higher in religion—there is, in effect, nothing else; if you look for anything but more love, you are looking wide of the mark, you are getting out of the royal way.

—JOHN WESLEY

The truth is . . . that God is being revealed to us every day in those nearest to us, wherever we are.

—JOYCE RUPP

Behold, Lord, an empty vessel that needs to be filled. My Lord, fill it. I am weak in the faith; strengthen me. I am cold in love; warm me and make me fervent, that my love may go out to my neighbor.

—MARTIN LUTHER

The light [God] gives creates community and draws people together in joy, with love flowing from the depths of their souls and finding expression in constructive deeds—deeds that build up and never destroy.

—EBERHARD ARNOLD

belong to a village

It is grace, nothing but grace, that we are allowed to live in community with Christian brethren.

—DIETRICH BONHOEFFER

Grace means there is nothing I can do to make God love me more, and nothing I can do to make God love me less. It means that I, even I who deserve the opposite, am invited to take my place at the table in God's family.

—PHILIP YANCEY

Love . . . consists in this, that two solitudes protect and touch and greet each other.

—RAINER MARIA RILKE

It is easier to love people in a theoretical sense while on a mission trip or in the spotlight or when you get fringe benefits and it makes you feel good. Love is, by definition, putting others before yourself. That means caring about what they care about—before, above, and beyond what I care about.

— ELIZABETH M.MOSBO VERHAGE

Our love should stretch as widely across all space, and should be as equally distributed in every portion of it, as is the very light of the sun. —SIMONE WEIL

A community isn't just a place where people live under the same roof; that is a lodging house or a hotel. Nor is a community a work-team. Even less is it a nest of vipers! It is a place where everyone—or, let's be realistic, the majority!—is emerging from the shadows of egocentricity to the light of a real love.

—JEAN VANIER

Farms, families, and communities are forms of art, just as are poems, paintings, and symphonies. None of these things would exist if we did not make them. We can make them either well or poorly; this choice is another thing that we make. —WENDELL BERRY

The physical presence of other Christians is a source of incomparable joy and strength to the believer.

—DIETRICH BONHOEFFER

belong to a village

If you can learn a simple trick, . . . you'll get along a lot better with all kinds of folks. You never really understand a person until you consider things from his point of view.   —HARPER LEE

We have one another only through Christ, but through Christ we do have one another, wholly, and for all eternity.   —DIETRICH BONHOEFFER

The dream of God is that all creation will live together in peace and harmony and fulfillment. All parts of creation.   —VERNA DOZIER

We will not experience God if we leave those who make mistakes of *any* kind outside our love. Whether our love takes the form of service, prayer, or donations, we must treat everyone as our sister and brother.

—HUGH PRATHER

PART 4

DO THE RIGHT THING

DO THE RIGHT THING

Philosopher Albert Camus wrote, "Life is the sum of all your choices." He probably wasn't referring to the mundane choices in life, such as paper or plastic, baked or fried, caf or decaf. Instead, Camus was talking about those times when we must choose to act justly, keeping in mind what will benefit our world and humankind.

Our other option at those crossroads is to blindly follow whatever seems to make us (or our friends or our country) happy. What is required of us when we face those kinds of choices? God makes it pretty clear: "I place before you Life and Death, Blessing and Curse. Choose life . . ." (Deut. 30:19, THE MESSAGE). Or, in modern vernacular, do the right thing.

It is the ability to choose which makes us human.

—MADELEINE L'ENGLE

Those who dare not say an ill-natured word or do an unreasonable thing because they consider God as everywhere present perform a better devotion than those who dare not miss church.

—WILLIAM LAW

Choose well: your choice is brief and yet endless.

—ELLA WINTER

Beloved, do not imitate what is evil but imitate what is good. Whoever does good is from God; whoever does evil has not seen God.   —3 JOHN 11 (NRSV)

Live *love*. Act *truth*. Honor *life*. And it will be God within you whom you live, act, and honor. God will not come to you because you have become "good." He was already there.   —CARLO CARRETTO

do the right thing

Christianity might be a good thing if anyone ever tried it.

—GEORGE BERNARD SHAW

[Humans] will wrangle for religion, write for it, fight for it, die for it, anything but live for it.

—CHARLES CALEB COTTON

Believe in the Lord and love him. Keep yourselves from impure thoughts and fleshly pleasures. Pray continually. Avoid vanity. Sing psalms before sleep and on awaking. Hold in your heart the commandments of scripture.

—ANTHONY

The most painful moral struggles are not those between good and evil, but between the good and the lesser good.

—BARBARA GRIZZUTI HARRISON

No trumpets sound when the important decisions of our life are made. Destiny is made known silently.

—AGNES DE MILLE

Father, if you are willing, remove this cup from me; yet, not my will but yours be done.

—JESUS, IN LUKE 22:42 (NRSV)

A spiritual life is simply a life in which all that we do comes from the centre, where we are anchored in God: a life soaked through and through by a sense of [God's] reality and claim, and self-given to the great movement of [God's] will.   —EVELYN UNDERHILL

Sins, however great and detestable they may be, are looked upon as trivial, or as not sins at all, when people get accustomed to them.   —AUGUSTINE

Conduct is more convincing than language.

—JOHN WOOLMAN

A humble farmer who serves God is better than a proud philosopher, who, neglecting himself, contemplates the course of the heavens.   —THOMAS À KEMPIS

do the right thing

I used to be Snow White, but I drifted.

—MAE WEST

I think there is an immense shortage of Christian charity among so-called Christians.

—HARRY S. TRUMAN

Happy are those whose greatest desire is to do what God requires; God will satisfy them fully!

—JESUS, IN MATTHEW 5:6 (GNT)

It is important to be straightforward and honest about your true feelings. Rather be too rude than too smooth, too blunt than too kind. Rather say an unkind word that is true than one that is "nice" but ungenuine. You can always be sorry for an unkind word, but hypocrisy causes permanent harm. —J. HEINRICH ARNOLD

Only the young die good. —ETHEL WATTS MUMFORD

We are raised up from the earth by two wings—simplicity and purity. There must be simplicity in our intention and purity in our desires. Simplicity leads to God; purity embraces and enjoys God.

—THOMAS À KEMPIS

When I was young and free and my imagination had no limits, I dreamed of changing the world. As I grew older and wiser, I discovered the world would not change, so I shortened my sights somewhat and decided to change only my country. But it too seemed immovable. As I grew into my twilight years, in one last desperate attempt, I settled for changing only my family, those closest to me, but alas they would have none of it. And now as I lie on my deathbed, I suddenly realize: *If I had only changed myself first, then by example I would have changed my family.* From their inspiration and encouragement, I would then have been able to better my country and who knows, I may have even changed the world.

—WRITTEN ON THE TOMB OF AN ANGLICAN BISHOP (1100 CE) IN THE CRYPTS OF WESTMINSTER ABBEY

do the right thing

Kindness is always fashionable.

—AMELIA E. BARR

You are the light of the world—but only because you are enkindled, made radiant by the One Light of the World. And being kindled, we have got to get on with it, be useful. —EVELYN UNDERHILL

Justice is not cheap. Justice is not quick. It is not ever finally achieved. —MARIAN WRIGHT EDELMAN

When you give love, more flows through you, and it becomes a special, special thing. And when you start living your life like that, about giving and not taking, and about caring, and being unselfish and not even thinking of yourself, you'd be amazed how beautiful life is.

—SAMMY HAGAR

Spirituality means to me living the ordinary life extraordinarily well. —WILLIAM SLOANE COFFIN

Many words do not satisfy the soul; but a good life eases the mind and a clean conscience inspires great trust in God. —THOMAS À KEMPIS

What do we live for, if it is not to make life less difficult to each other? —GEORGE ELIOT

If you go against the grain, you get splinters, regardless of which neighborhood you're from, what your parents taught you, what schools you attended. But if you embrace the way God does things, there are wonderful payoffs. —ROMANS 2:9-10 (THE MESSAGE)

To lend each other a hand when we're falling. . . . Perhaps that's the only work that matters in the end. —FREDERICK BUECHNER

Let your light shine before others, so that they may see your good works, and give glory to your Father in heaven. —MATTHEW 5:16 (NRSV)

do the right thing

I can resist everything except temptation.

—OSCAR WILDE

May God grant us the wisdom to discover right, the will to choose it, and the strength to make it endure.

—KING ARTHUR, IN *FIRST KNIGHT* (FILM, 1995)

The LORD has told us what is good. What he requires of us is this: to do what is just, to show constant love, and to live in humble fellowship with our God.

—MICAH 6:8 (GNT)

84

There is no need to be peculiar in order to find God.

—EVELYN UNDERHILL

The more you know and the better you understand, the more severely will you be judged, unless your life is also the more holy. Do not be proud, therefore, because of your learning or skill. Rather, fear because of the talent given you.

—THOMAS À KEMPIS

Maybe I would have a more positive view of religion if I was impressed by the behavior of those who preach it.

—TOM MORELLO OF RAGE AGAINST THE MACHINE

The greatest thing is to give thanks for everything. He who has learned this knows what it means to live. He has penetrated the whole mystery of life.

—ALBERT SCHWEITZER

You seem a little wealthy to be a servant of God, don't you think? —JOAN OF ARC, IN *MESSENGER: THE STORY OF JOAN OF ARC* (FILM, 1993)

Calm that excessive thirst for knowledge, for there is great discord and deception in it.

—THOMAS À KEMPIS

The truly happy life at all its points of contact with the world does not ask for anything; it gives something.

—PERCY C. AINSWORTH

do the right thing

Integrity pays, but not in cash.

—JENNIFER STONE

As long as [we are] looking for pay for what [we do], or want to get from God anything that God could or would give, [we are] like the merchants. If you want to be rid of the commercial spirit, do all you can in the way of good works, solely for the praise of God.

—MEISTER ECKHART

Don't let anyone put you down because you're young. Teach believers with your life: by word, by demeanor, by love, by faith, by integrity.

—1 TIMOTHY 4:12 (THE MESSAGE)

Practice confession—between you and God, between you and other people. It is a bridge that spans the chasms of hurt, pain, and wrongdoing. It is the bridge that leads to peace.

—HELEN R. NEINAST AND THOMAS C. ETTINGER

Stop asking God to bless what you're doing. Find out what God's doing. It's already blessed.

—BONO

Our task should not be to invoke religion and the name of God by claiming God's blessing and endorsement for all our national policies and practices—saying, in effect, that God is on our side. Rather, we should worry earnestly whether we are on God's side.

—ABRAHAM LINCOLN

I can laugh at a silly joke or even a gross joke or anything. When it gets into pornography, when it gets into things that I think are too off-color, then I start remembering, *Hey, I'm representing Christ here.*

—ALICE COOPER

Anyone who wishes to understand Christ's words and to savor them fully should strive to become like him in every way. —THOMAS À KEMPIS

do the right thing

In Christ's family there can be no division into Jew and non-Jew, slave and free, male and female. Among us you are all equal. —GALATIANS 3:28 (THE MESSAGE)

Your eyes are windows into your body. If you open your eyes wide in wonder and belief, your body fills up with light. If you live squinty-eyed in greed and distrust, your body is a dank cellar. If you pull the blinds on your windows, what a dark life you will have!

—MATTHEW 6:22-23 (THE MESSAGE)

Our fellowship with God issues in world concern. We cannot keep the love of God to ourselves. It spills over. It quickens us. It makes us see the world's needs anew.

—THOMAS R. KELLY

The Bible will not tell you whom to marry . . . , whom to vote for or which church to attend. However, it will help you become wise enough in the ways of God to make good decisions in those areas.

—KAREN LEE-THORP

The battle with sin is not an incident in the Christian life; it is the abiding condition of it.

—Percy C. Ainsworth

Only a few things are important in this life—and being right about a certain doctrine or truth is often not one of them.

—Doug Van Pelt

Grow up. You're kingdom subjects. Now live like it. Live out your God-created identity. Live generously and graciously toward others, the way God lives toward you.

—Matthew 5:48 (The Message)

Sometimes we need to *see* the Christian life lived out; we need to stand in the presence of the genuine article, not just be told about it.

—Timothy Jones

Happy are those who are concerned for the poor; the Lord will help them when they are in trouble.

—Psalm 41:1 (GNT)

do the right thing

Be sure that you first preach by the way you live. If you do not, people will notice that you say one thing, but live otherwise, and your words will bring only cynical laughter.

—CHARLES BORROMEO

You have upheld me because of my integrity, and set me in your presence forever.

—PSALM 41:12 (NRSV)

There is something really wonderful about the concept of frequently and rhythmically setting aside time for attention to the dearer things of life and for the deep and cleansing regeneration that we all require.

—WENDY M. WRIGHT

The riches and beauty of the spiritual landscape are not disclosed to us in order that we may sit in the sun parlour, be grateful for the excellent hospitality, and contemplate the glorious view. Some people suppose that the spiritual life mainly consists in doing that.

—EVELYN UNDERHILL

part 4

Your scientists were so preoccupied with whether or not they could, they didn't stop to think if they should.
—JEFF GOLDBLUM, IN *JURASSIC PARK*
(FILM, 1993)

If we have faith enough to remove mountains and do it only to show our power, rather than to show that divine Love is flowing through us, we gain nothing and are nothing.
—MORTON KELSEY

The real battle, the big struggle of our times, is the fundamental choice between cynicism and hope. The choice between cynicism and hope is ultimately a spiritual choice, and one that has enormous political consequences.
—JIM WALLIS

God's trust makes us eager to do right. Such is the genius of grace. The law can show us where we do wrong, but it can't make us eager to do right. Grace can.
—MAX LUCADO

do the right thing

Whoever walks with the wise becomes wise.

—Proverbs 13:20 (NRSV)

A Christian is not someone who merely admires or
believes in Christ, but one who does what [Christ] does.

—David Yount

American Christians drive me crazy. There are so many
of them, and they are so diverse. They are so loud
about unimportant things and so silent on important
ones.

—Kyle Matthews

Unless life and prayer are integrated, prayer becomes
unreal and life unsatisfying. If the gap between the two
becomes too wide, both go bad.

—Olive Wyon

A prayerful life . . . is one in which we convert the
world from darkness, people from mere roles to
persons.

—Henri J. M. Nouwen

May I speak each day according to thy justice,
Each day may I show thy chastening, O God;
May I speak each day according to thy wisdom,
Each day and night may I be at peace with thee.

—"DESIRES," *CARMINA GADELICA*

Blessed are the pure in heart, for they will see God.

—MATTHEW 5:8 (NRSV)

Thus says the LORD: Stand at the crossroads, and look,
and ask for the ancient paths, where the good way lies;
and walk in it, and find rest for your souls.

—JEREMIAH 6:16 (NRSV)

Ironically, sometimes the most basic struggles are the
most important ones.   —ELIZABETH M. MOSBO VERHAGE

No good deed will go unpunished.

—CLARE BOOTHE LUCE

93

do the right thing

A leader is someone with the power to project either shadow or light onto some part of the world and onto the lives of the people who dwell there. . . . A *good* leader is intensely aware of the interplay of inner shadow and light, lest the act of leadership do more harm than good. —PARKER J. PALMER

Balancing competing claims, working through all the implications of your position on an issue, being able to hear truth in the argument of someone with whom you disagree—this is the stuff of morality. You must pay attention to all these dynamics in order to build an ethical foundation that is strong and consistent—one that will empower you to "do the right thing." —THOMAS ETTINGER AND HELEN NEINAST

Let the mind of God descend over you, and disappear within it. —HUGH PRATHER

PART 5

EMBRACE YOUR DRAMA

EMBRACE YOUR DRAMA

Hard times are just . . . hard. Live long enough, and you'll experience that truth firsthand. Suffering is an inevitable part of the human experience.

Since we can't avoid pain, it's important to figure out how best to respond to it. When hard times come to us, do we rail against the injustice of it all? Or do we panic, thinking the universe is mean and irrational?

Another response to pain is to embrace it and learn from it. When we embrace our drama, we pick up insights that help us correct our course in life and teach us who we really are meant to be. If we want to live a good life, staying with our pain long enough to learn from it will make all the difference.

Suffering has always been with us; does it really matter in what form it comes? All that matters is how we bear it and how we fit it into our lives.

—Etty Hillesum

True knowledge comes only through suffering.

—Elizabeth Barrett Browning

I do not believe that sheer suffering teaches. If suffering alone taught, all the world would be wise, since everyone suffers. To suffering must be added mourning, understanding, patience, love, openness, and the willingness to remain vulnerable.

—Anne Morrow Lindbergh

Give your entire attention to what God is doing right now, and don't get worked up about what may or may not happen tomorrow. God will help you deal with whatever hard things come up when the time comes.

—Matthew 6:34 (The Message)

Any religion has to have a practice. When you let it go so far from practice that it just becomes a matter of talk, something bad happens. —WENDELL BERRY

Sometimes I wonder, when it gets too quiet up there, if you [God] are thinking, *What kind of mischief can I play on my friend Tevye?*
—TEVYE, IN *FIDDLER ON THE ROOF* (FILM, 1971)

Many of us grew up with a picture of what life would look like, even if it was an idealized picture. But now all we have are torn fragments of our pictures.
—KENT IRA GROFF

Sometimes what you want to do has to fail so *you* won't.
—MARGUERITTE HARMON BRO

Art by its nature is a transgressive act, and artists must accept being punished for it.
—JOYCE CAROL OATES

Failure is just another way to learn how to do
something right.　　　　　　—MARIAN WRIGHT EDELMAN

You're blessed when your commitment to God
provokes persecution. The persecution drives you
even deeper into God's kingdom.
　　　　　　　　　—MATTHEW 5:10 (THE MESSAGE)

Faith is not making religious-sounding noises in the
daytime. It is asking your inmost self questions at
night—and then getting up and going to work.
　　　　　　　　　　　—MARY JEAN IRION

99

Lord, how thou dost afflict thy lovers!
　　　　　　　　　　—TERESA OF AVILA

When God make cripple, he mean him to be lonely.
Nighttime, daytime, he got to travel that lonesome road.
Nighttime, daytime, he gotta travel that lonesome road.
　　　　—PORGY, IN *PORGY AND BESS* (VIDEO, 1993)

Pain is like a glass wall. It is impossible to climb it, but you must, and, somehow, you do. Then there is an explosion of brilliance, and the world is more apparent in its complexity and beauty.

—SUZANNE MASSIE

Sometime, whether or not you want it, you will have to part with everything. Cling, therefore, to Jesus in life and death. Trust yourself to the glory of the only One who can help you when all others fail.

—THOMAS À KEMPIS

I longed for honors, financial gain, marriage; and you mocked me. In these desires I underwent the bitterest hardships. You were more gracious the less you allowed anything that was not you to grow sweet to me.

—AUGUSTINE

The LORD is my light and my salvation; whom shall I fear? The LORD is the stronghold of my life; of whom then should I go in dread? —PSALM 27:1 (NEB)

If we would walk in the light and receive the life of grace, the way [Christ] teaches us to follow—his way— is to go the path of suffering, the path of disgrace, derision, torment, ridicule, and persecution. It is by such suffering that we become conformed with Christ crucified.

—CATHERINE OF SIENA

Those who've never rebelled against God or at some point in their lives shaken their fists in the face of heaven, have never encountered God at all.

—CATHERINE MARSHALL

The dark night of the soul exists for the sole purpose of furthering love. —GERALD G. MAY

The readiest way to escape from our sufferings is to be willing that they should endure as long as God pleases. . . . One of the greatest evidences of God's love to those who love him is to send them afflictions, with grace to bear them. —JOHN WESLEY

embrace your drama

Obstacles are a sign that God is pleased with something. The weakness of human means is a cause of strength to him. God uses adverse winds to blow us into port.

—CHARLES DE FOUCAULD

Without your wound where would your power be? . . . The very angels themselves cannot persuade the wretched and blundering children on earth as can one human being broken on the wheels of living. In Love's service, only the wounded soldiers can serve.

—THORNTON WILDER

It's a difficult business, being human.

—WENDELL BERRY

Religion . . . has tended to create people who think they have God in their pockets, people with quick, easy, glib answers. . . . If the great mystery is indeed the Great Mystery, it will lead us into paradox, into darkness, into journeys that never cease. —RICHARD ROHR

Everything can be taken from a [person] but . . . the last of the human freedoms—to choose one's attitude in any given set of circumstances. —Viktor Frankl

It's true that we [the Jews] are the Chosen People. But once in a while, can't you choose someone else?
—Tevye speaking to God,
in *Fiddler on the Roof*

Anyone who wants to live all out for Christ is in for a lot of trouble; there's no getting around it.
—2 Timothy 3:12 (The Message)

The great challenge is *living* your wounds through instead of *thinking* them through. It is better to cry than to worry, better to feel your wounds deeply than to understand them, better to let them enter into your silence than to talk about them.

—Henri J. M. Nouwen

When to all outward appearances others give us no credit, when they do not think well of us, then we are more inclined to seek God, who sees our hearts. Therefore, we ought to root ourselves so firmly in God that we will not need human consolations.

—THOMAS À KEMPIS

[Jesus] said to me, "My grace is sufficient for you, for power is made perfect in weakness." So, I will boast all the more gladly of my weaknesses, so that the power of Christ may dwell in me. Therefore I am content with weaknesses, insults, hardships, persecutions, and calamities for the sake of Christ; for whenever I am weak, then I am strong.

—2 CORINTHIANS 12:9-10 (NRSV)

I look up to the mountains;
does my strength come from mountains?
No, my strength comes from GOD,
Who made heaven, and earth, and mountains.

—PSALM 121:1-2 (THE MESSAGE)

part 5

To despair is to turn your back on God.

—MARILLA CUTHBERT, IN
ANNE OF GREEN GABLES (FILM, 1986)

As the Good Book says, "If you spit in the air, it lands in your face."   —TEVYE, IN *FIDDLER ON THE ROOF*

Our daily sorrows are anchored in a greater sorrow and therefore a larger hope. Absolutely nothing in our lives lies outside the realm of God's judgment and mercy.

—HENRI J. M. NOUWEN

God . . . he's bloody deaf, him.

—GEOFF TIPPS, IN *THE LEAGUE OF GENTLEMEN*
(TELEVISION SHOW, 1999)

[Christ] did not say: You will not be assailed, you will not be belabored, you will not be disquieted, but he said: You will not be overcome.

—JULIAN OF NORWICH

embrace your drama

Come to me, all you who are weary and burdened, and I will give you rest. —Jesus, in Matthew 11:28 (NIV)

Let us run with perseverance the race that is set before us, looking to Jesus the pioneer and perfecter of our faith, who for the sake of the joy that was set before him endured the cross, disregarding its shame, and has taken his seat at the right hand of the throne of God.

Consider him who endured such hostility against himself from sinners, so that you may not grow weary or lose heart. —Hebrews 12:1-3 (NRSV)

The first and final deliverance from trouble is not by the path of explanation; it is by the path of faith.

—Percy C. Ainsworth

Our friends are all those who unjustly afflict upon us trials and ordeals, shame and injustice, sorrows and torments, martyrdom and death. We must love them greatly, for we will possess eternal life because of what they bring upon us. —Francis of Assisi

Why are you cast down, O my soul, and why are you disquieted within me? Hope in God; for I shall again praise him, my help and my God.

—Psalm 42:11 (NRSV)

Where the hell is this God of yours?

—Lieutenant Daniel Taylor, in
Forrest Gump (film, 1994)

Our foe is shut up within ourselves.

—John Cassian

There is a deep sense in which the joys of life are its ripened sorrows.　—Percy C. Ainsworth

Ironically, the more we grow in the spirit of Jesus Christ, the poorer we become. The more we realize that everything is gift, the more the tenor of our life becomes one of humble, joyful thanksgiving.

—Brennan Manning

Jesus' life didn't go well. He didn't reach his earning potential. He didn't have the respect of his colleagues. His friends weren't loyal. His life wasn't long. He didn't meet his soul mate. And he wasn't understood by his mother. Yet I think I deserve all those things because I am spiritual. —HUGH PRATHER

Waiting is one of the most difficult and most divine aspects of our experience. —ELIZABETH J. CANHAM

Winter is a season of some very real losses. The flowers of springtime are gone; leaves fall. Trees stand bare and revealed. However, from these losses there are gifts to be had. —KATHLEEN FISCHER

The grace of God has found space in my life in the empty, hollowed-out spaces in my heart, not in the parts of my life that I have managed to fill up with my own "achievements." —MARGARET SILF

part 5

A simple faith supports us in the valley; but . . . during the long climb up the mountain side we are being trained into a much stronger faith in God. We are learning to believe where we cannot see, and we are sure that there is light at the top.

—OLIVE WYON

All creatures that have wings can escape from every snare that is set for them, if only they will fly high enough; and the soul that uses its wings can always find a sure "way to escape" from all that can hurt or trouble it.   —HANNAH WHITALL SMITH

God can handle it.   —JOHN KILLINGER

Most of us have experienced wilderness places along the way of our faith journey, times of solitude when God spoke tenderly to us as well as moments of intense pain and loss that seemed barren. Deserts sometimes come to us unbidden.   —ELIZABETH J. CANHAM

embrace your drama

Winter does not go easily away, yet venturesome birds sing the song of resurrection in the fresh mornings.

—W. PAUL JONES

Grace strikes us when we are in great pain and restlessness. It strikes us when we walk through the dark valley of a meaningless and empty life. . . . Sometimes at that moment a wave of light breaks into our darkness, and it is as though a voice were saying: "You are accepted."

—PAUL TILLICH

Altho' today [God] prunes my twigs with pain,
Yet doth his blood nourish and warm my root:
Tomorrow I shall put forth buds again
And clothe myself with fruit.

—CHRISTINA ROSSETTI

We should not be surprised when we see human suffering and pain all around us. But we should be surprised by joy every time we see that God, not the Evil One, has the last word. —HENRI J. M. NOUWEN

part 5

The wish to pray is a prayer in itself.

—GEORGES BERNANOS

The suffering and sin of the world can be effectively confronted only with grace. Opening ourselves to the world's brokenness before arming ourselves with the resources God makes available can lead not to a rich spiritual life but to discouragement and despair.

—GREGORY S. CLAPPER

III

Is there any wonder that deeper than idea and concept is the insistent conviction that the night can never stay, that winter is ever moving toward the spring?

—HOWARD THURMAN

If there be anywhere on earth a lover of God who is always kept safe from falling, I know nothing of it, for it was not shown me. But this was shown: that whether in falling or in rising we are always kept in the same precious love.

—JULIAN OF NORWICH

embrace your drama

Salvation is free, but the cost of discipleship is enormous.   —RUEBEN P. JOB

No faith is so precious as that which lives and triumphs in adversity. Tried faith brings experience. You could not have believed your own weakness had you not been compelled to pass through the rivers; and you would never have known God's strength had you not been supported amid the water-floods.

—CHARLES H. SPURGEON

If we, too, would become people of prayer, . . . we must expect our pathway to God to take us through the desert.   —JOYCE HUGGETT

Perhaps we are more attentive when life is hard. When we are open and vulnerable, the Spirit can more easily lead us forth to fuller expressions of wisdom, compassion, and love—to the heart of our humanity, the *imago dei*, the image of God.   —JEAN M. BLOMQUIST

part 5

We do not yet live in the realized sovereign realm of God on earth. Our journeys as individuals, as communities, still pass through hard and dangerous places, places that may very well look and act like wilderness.

But here is the gift, here is the promise, here is the grace for our wilderness: God will journey with us.

—JOHN INDERMARK

Faith is the deep confidence that God is good and that God's goodness somehow triumphs.

—HENRI J. M. NOUWEN

Let it be.   —PAUL McCARTNEY

The humiliation that brings us down—down to ground on which it is safe to stand and to fall—eventually takes us to a firmer and fuller sense of self. When people ask me how it felt to emerge from depression, I can give only one answer: I felt at home in my own skin, and at home on the face of the earth, for the first time.

—PARKER J. PALMER

embrace your drama

Sometimes one has simply to endure a period of
depression for what it may hold of illumination if
one can live through it, attentive to what it exposes
or demands. —MAY SARTON

Somehow losing myself helped me find my truer self;
losing love helped me learn to love more fully and
authentically; failing in relationship taught me much
about being in relationship in a creative, nurturing way;
and experiencing broken trust revealed how precious
life is with someone who is worthy of trust. Out of my
deepest pain has arisen my greatest joy.
—JEAN M. BLOMQUIST

We are walking in a ticker tape parade. . . . Some pieces
of confetti read "great calves," some "chronic sinus,"
some "no noticeable hair loss," some "multiple
sclerosis." . . . Don't judge your neighbor by what
pieces of paper fall on his or her shoulders. Don't think
you are cursed or "blessed" by what pieces fall on yours.
—HUGH PRATHER

PART 6

GO FOR BROKE

GO FOR BROKE

When facing life-altering decisions, such as what kind of work to do, whether and whom to marry, and where to live, we often must choose between safety or risk. Sometimes safety is the right choice, as when we decide against building a house at the base of a live volcano. Other times, taking a risk, even though it is scary is the life-giving choice.

Faith, believing what God said, almost always requires risk. The Bible is full of examples of people who chose risk over safety. Imagine seventy-five-year-old Abraham pondering whether to go for broke—to obey God and leave home with his large family, not knowing where they would end up and how they would survive.

Risk taking is not for the foolish or the faint of heart. It should not be done without good reason. But when taking a risk is truly called for, and we find the courage to take the leap, we find ourselves on the other side, shaky and a bit winded, but feeling more alive than we have in years.

If you're never scared or embarrassed or hurt, it means you never take any chances. —Julia Sorel

To change one's life: Start immediately. Do it flamboyantly. No exceptions. —William James

There is always an enormous temptation in all of life to diddle around. . . . I won't have it. The world is wilder than that in all directions, more dangerous and bitter, more extravagant and bright. We are making hay when we should be making whoopee; we are raising tomatoes when we should be raising Cain, or Lazarus.

—Annie Dillard

How cool, how quiet is true courage!

—Fanny Burney

Nobody is ever met at the airport when beginning a new adventure. It's just not done.

—Elizabeth Warnock Fernea

go for broke

Death twitches my ear. "Live," he says, "I am coming."

—Virgil

[God's love] squeezes in through the tiniest of openings, refracts throughout your entire inner self, and drives out the fear and anxieties that prevent you from becoming who you are.

—E. Glenn Hinson

Risk! Risk anything! Care no more for the opinions of others, for those voices. Do the hardest thing on earth for you. Act for yourself. Face the truth.

—Katherine Mansfield

Keep yourself as a stranger here on earth, a pilgrim whom its affairs do not concern at all. Keep your heart free and raise it up to God, for you have not here a lasting home.

—Thomas à Kempis

Between two evils, I always pick the one I never tried before.

—Mae West

We can say with confidence, "The Lord is my helper; I will not be afraid. What can anyone do to me?"

—HEBREWS 13:6 (NRSV)

How can God direct our steps if we're not taking any?

—SARAH LEAH GRAFSTEIN

Just because I'm so horribly conditioned to accept everybody else's values, and just because I like applause and people to rave about me, doesn't make it right. I'm ashamed of it. I'm sick of it. I'm sick of not having the courage to be an absolute nobody.

—J. D. SALINGER

It is madness to wear . . . hats to church; we should all be wearing crash helmets. Ushers should issue life preservers and signal flares; they should lash us to our pews. For the sleeping god may wake someday and take offense, or the waking god may draw us out to where we can never return.

—ANNIE DILLARD

go for broke

I have the sense that part of what it means to be human is that, on this side of Jordan, even on my best days I will always feel a little homesick for intimacy with my Creator. —KYLE MATTHEWS

I love the recklessness of faith. First you leap, and then you grow wings. —WILLIAM SLOANE COFFIN

The fullness of life is in the hazards of life.
—EDITH HAMILTON

Know! A person walks in life
on a very narrow bridge.
The most important thing
is not to be afraid. —REBBE NACHMAN OF BRESLOV

Don't panic. I'm with you. There's no need to fear, for I'm your God. I'll give you strength. I'll help you. I'll hold you steady, keep a firm grip on you.
—ISAIAH 41:10 (THE MESSAGE)

If we only have so many days on earth, then we should, like the inmates in the movie *The Shawshank Redemption*, see that this leaves us only two options: "Get busy living or get busy dying."

—GREGORY S. CLAPPER

To escape criticism—do nothing, say nothing, be nothing.

—ELBERT HUBBARD

Liberation, whether experienced pleasurably or painfully, always involves relinquishment, some kind of *loss.*

—GERALD G. MAY

God uses people like you, Lancelot. Because your heart is open. You hold nothing back. You give all of yourself.

—ARTHUR, IN *FIRST KNIGHT*
(FILM, 1995)

I don't think. I leave that to God. I'm just a messenger in all of this.

—JOAN OF ARC

Sometimes we have to step into the sea before the waters will be parted. —MAXIE DUNNAM

The human soul has need of security and also of risk. The fear of violence or of hunger or of any other extreme evil is a sickness of the soul. The boredom produced by a complete absence of risk is also a sickness of the soul. —SIMONE WEIL

If your prayer is not enticing you outside your comfort zones, if your Christ is not an occasional "threat," you probably need to do some growing up and learning to love. —RICHARD ROHR

When we give ourselves to spiritual journeying, we soon realize that God always invites us beyond where we are. —SUE MONK KIDD

Keep alert, stand firm in your faith, be courageous, be strong. —1 CORINTHIANS 16:13 (NRSV)

part 6

Prayer is . . . a very dangerous business. For all the benefits it offers of growing closer to God, it carries with it one great element of risk: the possibility of change. In prayer we open ourselves to the chance that God will do something with us that we had not intended.

—EMILIE GRIFFIN

When Christ calls [us], he bids [us] come and die.

—DIETRICH BONHOEFFER

Only in growth, reform, and change, paradoxically enough, is true security to be found.

—ANNE MORROW LINDBERGH

This impotence of "systems" is a main reason why Jesus did not send his students out to start governments or even churches as we know them today. . . . They were, instead, to establish beachheads of his person, word, and power in the midst of a failing and futile humanity.

—DALLAS WILLARD

go for broke

Why can't we treat death with a certain amount of humanity and dignity, and decency, and God forbid, maybe even humor? Death is not the enemy, gentlemen. If we're going to fight a disease, let's fight one of the most terrible diseases of all: indifference.

—PATCH ADAMS, IN *PATCH ADAMS*
(FILM, 1998)

God did not give us a spirit of cowardice, but rather a spirit of power and of love and of self-discipline.

—2 TIMOTHY 1:7 (NRSV)

You pray inwardly, "Take all of me, take all of me."

—THOMAS R. KELLY

Please pray for me, that I may have both spiritual and physical strength to perform my duties; that I may not only speak the truth, but become the truth; that I may not only be called a Christian, but also live like a Christian.

—IGNATIUS OF ANTIOCH

part 6

Here is my life; here is my honor; here is my will; I have given them all to you; I am yours; do with me what you will. —TERESA OF AVILA

The place to improve the world is first in one's own heart and head and hands. —ROBERT M. PIRSIG

Is life so wretched? Isn't it rather your hands which are too small, your vision which is muddied? You are the one who must grow up. —DAG HAMMARSKJÖLD

The most difficult step in the Christian life is the one we do not want to take but must take anyway because it is God's will. —MARY ANNA VIDAKOVICH

The saints differ from us in their exuberance, the excess of our human talents. Moderation is not their secret. It is in the wildness of their dreams, the desperate vitality of their ambitions, that they stand apart from ordinary people of good will. —PHYLLIS MCGINLEY

The secret of quiet confidence in a world that furnishes us with the sight of so many sad things does not lie in shutting our eyes. That is the expedient of the cowardly and the faithless. It lies in looking at things as they are, and letting the sad vision force us back upon the mercy and power of God.

—PERCY C. AINSWORTH

Trust is a form of vision. It sees the fog or the unbroken stretch of tundra not as sterile and repellent but as personal, mysterious, and beckoning.

—MIRIAM POLLARD

God's works are perfect in every stage of their growth.

—HANNAH WHITALL SMITH

I invite you to believe that this God who has been "messing around" in your life knows you, loves you, and wants to help you find the meaning of your life. This daring risk of faith may sound strange to you, but go ahead and take the leap.

—BEN CAMPBELL JOHNSON

I reckon my own life to be worth nothing to me; I only
want to complete my mission and finish the work that
the Lord Jesus gave me to do, which is to declare the
Good News about the grace of God.

—PAUL, IN ACTS 20:24 (GNT)

The soul that plays for safety, even spiritual safety,
never becomes perfect.   —EVELYN UNDERHILL

You choose hope, not as a naive wish, but as a choice,
with your eyes wide open to the reality of the world—
just like the cynics who have not made the decision for
hope.   —JIM WALLIS

The purpose of prayer, the sacraments, and spiritual
disciplines is to awaken us.   —THOMAS KEATING

Let us therefore approach the throne of grace with
boldness, so that we may receive mercy and find grace
to help in time of need.   —HEBREWS 4:16 (NRSV)

go for broke

Spiritual development is a journey through the desert. There will be few trees to shade us and few oases to quench our thirst. The presence of a desert will discourage some people from making the journey because the way is hard and the route uncertain. It is easy to get lost. Therefore, it is absolutely essential that we travel light.

—WILLIAM O. PAULSELL

I wanted you to see what real courage is, instead of getting the idea that courage is a man with a gun in his hand. It's when you know you're licked before you begin, but you begin anyway and you see it through no matter what.

—HARPER LEE

The only thing that matters is wherever we go, wherever we grow, God undergirds us, God goes with us, God goes ahead of us, God will be there to welcome us!

—FLORA SLOSSON WUELLNER

Give your servants fearless confidence in preaching your Message.

—ACTS 4:29 (THE MESSAGE)

It costs so much to be a full human being . . . . One has
to abandon altogether the search for security, and
reach out to the risk of living with both arms. . . . One
has to accept pain as a condition of existence. One has
to count doubt and darkness as the cost of knowing.

—MORRIS WEST

No one's really got it all figured out just yet.

—ALANIS MORISSETTE

Nothing eases pain like embracing it, blessing it, and
expressing [it]. We can make the decision, no matter
how far gone we may think we are, to change our lives
and walk, talk, dress, eat, relate, love, and LIVE in ways
that draw to us the energy of wholeness and healing
into our lives.   —INDIA.ARIE

Christians are supposed not merely to endure change,
nor even to profit by it, but to cause it.

—HARRY EMERSON FOSDICK

go for broke

Try to live now in such a manner that at the moment of death you may be glad rather than fearful. Learn to die to the world now, that then you may begin to live with Christ. Learn to spurn all things now, that then you may freely go to him. —THOMAS À KEMPIS

Courage! I have shown it for years; think you I shall lose it at the moment when my sufferings are to end? —MARIE ANTOINETTE

Whatever you decide to do with your life will involve a small death inside of you, a giving over to something that was not there before and a leaving behind something that was once there. . . . Once you select what is most significant in your life, you walk away from less significant things, which makes you stronger but also makes you less of a child. —CHRISTOPHER DE VINCK

Never measure the height of a mountain, until you have reached the top. Then you will see how low it was. —DAG HAMMARSKJÖLD

part 6

Give it everything you have, heart and soul. Make sure you carry out The Revelation that Moses commanded you, every bit of it. Don't get off track, either left or right, so as to make sure you get to where you're going.

—JOSHUA 1:7 (THE MESSAGE)

The life of prayer is perhaps the most mysterious dimension of all human experience. We come to be at home with a God we cannot see. We discover that it is only by giving ourselves away totally that we truly come to possess ourselves, that we are most free when most surrendered. We begin to realize that light is darkness and darkness light.   —THOMAS H. GREEN

131

In danger there is great power.

—AGNES WHISTLING ELK

God took a great risk by announcing forgiveness in advance, and the scandal of grace involves a transfer of that risk to us.   —PHILIP YANCEY

go for broke

Be slow to pray. This is not an enterprise to be entered into lightly. When we pray we are using words that bring us into proximity with words that break cedars, shake the wilderness, make the oaks whirl, and strip forests bare. —EUGENE H. PETERSON

Avoiding danger is no safer in the long run than outright exposure. The fearful are caught as often as the bold. —HELEN KELLER

You become courageous by doing courageous acts. . . . Courage is a habit. —MARY DALY

Our love should stretch as widely across all space, and should be as equally distributed in every portion of it, as is the very light of the sun. —SIMONE WEIL

We should be willing to act as a balm for all wounds. —ETTY HILLESUM

Life shrinks or expands in proportion to one's courage.

—ANAÏS NIN

Security is when everything is settled, when nothing can happen to you; security is the denial of life.

—GERMAINE GREER

Never give up your ideas of beauty and goodness and passion. These are hints of heaven . . . on this earth; and if you can find people in your life who share this vision, you will be a lucky person indeed.

—CHRISTOPHER DE VINCK

Following Christ has nothing to do with success as the world sees success. It has to do with love.

—MADELEINE L'ENGLE

Do not be afraid of them, for I am with you to deliver you, says the LORD.   —JEREMIAH 1:8 (NRSV)

Surrender is not so much a giving up as it is an *opening up*. It is a dynamic living and striving in the face of the unknown. When we surrender in faith, we enter into the power of God, into the realm of all possibility.

—JEAN M. BLOMQUIST

If you risk nothing, then you risk everything.

—GEENA DAVIS

The time comes when you must make a leap of faith. You won't get there taking one small, safe, reasonable step after another. That got you to this point, but now you have a decision to make, and this time it has to be permanent.

—HUGH PRATHER

Forming a deep faith means intentionally choosing to jump into the current or flow of grace that runs through life. . . . One of the struggles of the faith journey is that . . . we never know what to expect.

—N. GRAHAM STANDISH

PART 7

SEE THE UNSEEN

SEE THE UNSEEN

Some things in life defy rational explanation. We've all heard of someone who is miraculously healed of a fatal disease, or of a mysterious letter that arrives on the day the rent is due containing exactly the amount of money needed. There are persons imprisoned for years by addictive behaviors who, astonishingly, one day are set free. Those are the dramatic miracles, the ones that get all the attention.

But there are other miracles, ones that are easy to miss: the gradual thawing of a cold heart, the mending of a long-broken relationship, the despair that is replaced one day by hope. As Macrina Wiederkehr says, these "small, daily miracles don't make the headlines, yet these are the real miracles."

Do we see the small miracles happening around us every day? There . . . see that? No? Maybe it's time to open our eyes and heart to a reality more real than the "real world." All it takes is training ourselves to look.

This whole world is full of God!

—BLESSED ANGELA OF FOLIGNO

Earth's crammed with heaven,
And every common bush afire with God.

—ELIZABETH BARRETT BROWNING

I do not feel the need to see all of God at once, to
comprehend God, as if I even could. It is enough for
me to have a few clear images of how God is. So long as
they resonate with scripture and with my experience
and so long as they produce in me the fruits of the
Spirit, . . . I will simply be grateful to have them with
me, as I seek daily to somehow become more like the
invisible God I serve.   —KYLE MATTHEWS

137

The preacher says that that sin's been warshed away
too. Neither God nor man's got nothin' on me now.
C'mon in, boys, the water is fine.

—DELMAR O'DONNELL, IN *O BROTHER,
WHERE ART THOU?* (FILM, 2000)

The world is full of miracles that most of us never see. We have not trained ourselves to look.

—JOHN KILLINGER

I think it pisses God off if you walk by the color purple in a field somewhere and don't notice it.

—ALICE WALKER

Faith, it seems to me, is not the holding of certain dogmas; it is simply openness and readiness of heart to believe any truth which God may show.

—MARGARET DELAND

When you consider God as acting in all things and all events, then all things will become holy to you, like miracles, and fill you with the same awe-filled sentiments of the divine presence.   —WILLIAM LAW

Miracles come after a lot of hard work.

—SUE BENDER

I would rather live in a world where my life is
surrounded by mystery than live in a world so small
that my mind could comprehend it.

—HARRY EMERSON FOSDICK

All the way to heaven is heaven.

—CATHERINE OF SIENA

The interior life is not a question of seeing
extraordinary things, but rather of seeing the ordinary
things with the eyes of God.   —THOMAS H. GREEN

Entrances to holiness are everywhere.
The possibility of ascent is all the time.
Even at unlikely times and through unlikely places.
There is no place on earth without the Presence.

—LAWRENCE KUSHNER

Life from the Center is a life of unhurried peace and
power.   —THOMAS R. KELLY

Becoming the Beloved means letting the truth of our Belovedness become enfleshed in everything we think, say, or do. It entails a long and painful process of appropriation or, better, incarnation.

—HENRI J. M. NOUWEN

[Saints] are flesh and blood, just like you and me, no stronger, no more intelligent. And that is the point. They simply offer themselves to God, knowing they are not the elite, fully cognizant that they are inadequate to the task, that their abilities are limited and fallible.

—JAMES C. HOWELL

Look for yourself, and you will find in the long run only hatred, loneliness, despair, rage, ruin, and decay. But look for Christ and you will find him, and with him everything else thrown in.

—C. S. LEWIS

Prayer does not demand that we interrupt our work, but that we continue working as if it were a prayer.

—MOTHER TERESA

part 7

God does not die on the day when we cease to believe in a personal deity, but we die on the day when our lives cease to be illumined by the steady radiance, renewed daily, of a wonder, the source of which is beyond all reason.　　　　　　—DAG HAMMARSKJÖLD

If Jesus were to come today, people would not even crucify him. They would ask him to dinner, and hear what he had to say, and make fun of him.

—THOMAS CARLYLE

We will only be happy in our reading of the Bible when we dare to approach it as the means by which God really speaks to us, the God who loves us and will not leave us with our questions unanswered.

—DIETRICH BONHOEFFER

It is not what you are nor what you have been that God looks at with his merciful eyes, but what you desire to be.　　　　　—*THE CLOUD OF UNKNOWING*

see the unseen

The mystery of forgiveness is the entire gospel. When you "get" forgiveness, you get it. . . . God forgives all things for being imperfect, broken, and poor. . . . The people who know God well—the mystics, the hermits, those who risk everything to find God—always meet a lover, not a dictator.   —RICHARD ROHR

A relationship with God is the true identity. After all, we are modeled after him, and he's our Creator.

—JOHN MAURER OF SOCIAL DISTORTION

Being a saint is simply being the person God made me to be. Saints, at the end of the day, are not really strange or odd or misfits. They are simply real, or normal. They actually are what we all are made to be, what we can be.

—JAMES C. HOWELL

Scripture is a treasure; it sets the heart free; it brings light and peace; it is sweeter than honey and becomes like songs even in places where the psalmist is not at home.   —ELIZABETH J. CANHAM

Oh, God, but it's good to be alive! The earth is like a field in summer, just bursting with good things. Someday, when all the wars are over, someone young will lead us to the harvest. As long as there are children, anything is possible.

—TSAR NICHOLAS II, IN *NICHOLAS AND ALEXANDRA* (FILM, 1971)

A poet is someone who is astonished by everything.

—ANONYMOUS

We do not think ourselves into new ways of living. We live ourselves into new ways of thinking.

—RICHARD ROHR

In those serendipitous moments when I get a glimpse of the hem of God's garment, or feel the peace of Christ, or experience the sense of family even when I'm far from home, I can tell that even my atoms have always known that my true home is wherever Jesus is.

—KYLE MATTHEWS

see the unseen

All I'm trying to say is, "I was one thing at one time, and I'm something new. I'm a new creature now. Don't judge Alice by what he used to be. Praise God for what I am now."   —Alice Cooper

Take off your sandals, for you are standing on holy ground.   —God speaking to Moses, Exodus 3:5 (nlt)

It is not enough to hear of Christ, or read of Christ; but this is the thing: to feel him my root, my life, my foundation; and my soul engrafted into him.
                                                                    —Isaac Penington

He departed from our eyes that we should return to our own hearts and find him there.

                                                                    —Augustine

We build around us pools of joy that we can fall into and swim when we are hot or tired or thirsty or when we feel that we just want to be young again and laugh.
                                                                    —Christopher de Vinck

There is no way of telling people that they are all
walking around shining like the sun.

—Thomas Merton

If I take the wings of the morning and settle at the
farthest limits of the sea, even there your hand shall
lead me, and your right hand shall hold me fast.

—Psalm 139:9-10 (nrsv)

Faith does more than hold [our] hand in the darkness; it
leads [us] into the light.   —Percy C. Ainsworth

Grant me the happiness of one whose life is each day
fresh and innocent and hopeful, each day pardoned.

—Michael Bouttier

Have you ever come on anything quite like this
extravagant generosity of God, this deep, deep wisdom?
It's way over our heads. We'll never figure it out.

—Romans 11:33 (The Message)

see the unseen

Listen to your life. See it for the fathomless mystery that it is. In the boredom and pain of it no less than in the excitement and gladness: touch, taste, smell your way to the holy and hidden heart of it because in the last analysis all moments are key moments, and life itself is grace. —FREDERICK BUECHNER

Your word is a lamp to my feet and a light to my path. —PSALM 119:105 (NRSV)

146

Mystics . . . fascinate us. They are so penetrated by the supernatural that they make visions appear to be as natural as visits with Grandma. They seem to be touched by the divine, and we also long for God to rest his hand upon us. —BERT GHEZZI

I am the Vine, you are the branches. When you're joined with me and I with you, the relation intimate and organic, the harvest is sure to be abundant. Separated, you can't produce a thing.

—JESUS, IN JOHN 15:5 (THE MESSAGE)

part 7

You have changed my sadness into a joyful dance;
you have taken away my sorrow and surrounded me
with joy.   —PSALM 30:11 (GNT)

Without Christ I was like a fish out of water, or like a
bird in the water. With Christ I am in the ocean of Love,
and while in the world, am in heaven.

—SUNDAR SINGH

Underneath the Creation are the words of life, "Let
there be . . . and there was." Underneath the Exodus
are words of deliverance. Underneath the wilderness,
words of judgment.

God's words are underneath everything. And if you
listen carefully, you will hear them.

—KEN GIRE

To grow spiritually is to become integrated and fulfilled
as a person. It is all the difference between being, in
the spiritual sense, a mixed-up pile of branches and
twigs and a living tree.   —MARJORIE WILKINSON

see the unseen

We are all more than we know, and that wondrous reality, that wholeness, holiness, is there for all of us, not the qualified only.

—MADELEINE L'ENGLE

When I look at the future, it's so bright, it burns my eyes.

—OPRAH WINFREY

Small miracles are all around us. We can find them everywhere—in our homes, in our daily activities, and, hardest to see, in ourselves. —SUE BENDER

Whoever questioned the beauty of the sunset? But who can define it? The astronomer can give us the mathematics of it. There doubtless is mathematics in the sunset; but there is no sunset glory in the mathematics. There is a chemistry of colours; but there is no wistful, healing light in that chemistry. Beauty defined is beauty destroyed. —PERCY C. AINSWORTH

I could be quite happy if I never read another book—if only I could reread those that had begun to shape my life and vision thus far. . . . What mattered most was not breadth but depth. I did not have to swallow the sea. I could relax and let the sea swallow me.

—THOMAS H. GREEN

The glory of God is a human being fully alive.

—IRENAEUS

149

Wherever we look, we see not only confusion but beauty. In snowflake, leaf, or insect, we discover structured patterns of a delicacy and balance that nothing manufactured by human skill can equal.

—KALLISTOS WARE

God is a stupendously rich reality—the alone bound-lessly rich Reality. His outward action throughout the universe—his creation, sustentation, and direction of the world at large—is immensely rich.

—FRIEDRICH VON HÜGEL

The whole universe is a perpetual miracle, and the most ordinary everyday events are as miraculous as the miracles at Lourdes. —ERNESTO CARDENAL

The revealing of the Holy One is what we need to transform our lives. We need to know that the ground on which we are standing is holy ground. When we have found one truly holy place, then all places become holy. —DAVID ADAM

When our wills are united with the will of God, we never take all the goodness and beauty and people and things in life for granted, but we accept them again and again as a gift from him—given that we may serve him with still greater joy and thank him for it. —ALBERT SCHWEITZER

For the sun meets not the springing bud that stretches towards him, with half that certainty, as God, the Source of all good, communicates himself to the soul that longs to partake of him. —WILLIAM LAW

To live gratefully re-lights my awareness and re-kindles
my love, for the capacity for true sight cannot really
be exercised apart from the practice of love—the
capacity to see with love and delight, with wonder
and tenderness, and above all with gratitude.

—ESTHER DE WAAL

[Joy] is the soul's just response to the rhythm of
righteousness.   —PERCY C. AINSWORTH

Creator of the world,
awaken me to the blessedness of earth,
that I may honor those who once dwelled
along these paths that I now travel.

—JAN L. RICHARDSON

Though you think yourselves ever so stupid, dull, and
incapable of sublime attainments, yet, by prayer, you
may live in God . . . with less difficulty or interruption
than you live in the vital air.

—MADAME GUYON

see the unseen

There is not one speck of beauty under the sun that does not mirror back the beauty of God.

—Roberta C. Bondi

I think the thrush's voice is more like God's than many a preacher's telling of the Word.

—Evelyn Underhill

We look for visions from heaven, for earthquakes and thunders of God's power (the fact that we are dejected proves that we do), and we never dream that all the time God is in the commonplace things and people around us.

—Oswald Chambers

Everything that happens has a meaning, and the ordinary is as meaningful as the miracle. A mouse is a miracle, as Walt Whitman says. Everything ordinary is a miracle, all the more marvelous because we do not pay attention to it. It is the humble unseen miracle of every day.

—Ernesto Cardenal

John, the messenger of God's Advent *then,* came in a most unlikely *place:* the wilderness. So let us not be surprised if God's Advent word continues to be heralded in out-of-the-way locales: soup kitchens, drug rehabilitation centers, halfway homes, in churches and institutions routinely overlooked and underestimated by everyone save the God who works life-changing activity there.
—JOHN INDERMARK

Almighty and everlasting God, you made the universe with all its marvelous order, its atoms, worlds, and galaxies, and the infinite complexity of living creatures: Grant that, as we probe the mysteries of your creation, we may come to know you more truly, and more surely fulfill our role in your eternal purpose; in the name of Jesus Christ our Lord. Amen.
—THE BOOK OF COMMON PRAYER

Miracles are God's *coup d'état.*
—ANNE-SOPHIE SWETCHINE

see the unseen

It is my experience that I find what I look for. I begin to notice what I am paying attention to—whether it be yellow crocuses bursting through the snow in March, or God's invitations to come and listen scattered throughout the Bible story. —WENDY MILLER

This is what theology is about. It is looking at reality with the eyes of God. And there is so much to look at: land and sky; sun, stars, and moon; women, men, and children; continents, countries, cities and towns.

—HENRI J. M. NOUWEN

The mysterious reign of God has begun. It is full of surprises. —MARY CATHERINE NOLAN

In every wind that blows, in every night and day of the year, in every sign of the sky, in every blossoming and in every withering of the earth, there is a real coming of God to us if we will simply use our starved imagination to realize it. —OSWALD CHAMBERS

The spiritual life has its seasons, one of which is winter.
. . . But beneath the appearance of lifelessness, God's love
continues to give life at deep levels.

—ROBERT F. MORNEAU

Our real need in life is not more time, but more eternity.

—PERCY C. AINSWORTH

Faith is a *habit.* Confidence comes from *habitual* faith. . . .
Christians gain confidence and motivation by "putting on
the mind of Christ"—breaking through their egos to see
themselves from God's point of view—*habitually.* In
other words, the confident Christian views life by the
light of faith. —DAVID YOUNT

Hope is willing to leave unanswered questions
unanswered and unknown futures unknown. Hope
makes you see God's guiding hand not only in the
gentle and pleasant moments but also in the shadows
of disappointment and darkness. —HENRI J. M. NOUWEN

Each day holds a surprise. But only if we expect it can we see, hear, or feel it when it comes to us. Let's not be afraid to receive each day's surprise, whether it comes to us as sorrow or as joy. —HENRI J. M. NOUWEN

As the earth drinks in the rain, as the sea receives the streams, as night accepts light from the stars, so we, giving nothing, partake freely of the grace of God.

—CHARLES H. SPURGEON

Being Christian is believing that life has a meaning, that everything, even sin, can turn to our benefit if we are not discouraged from loving. —LOUIS EVELY

For all that has been—Thanks!
To all that shall be—Yes! —DAG HAMMARSKJÖLD

To treat life as less than a miracle is to give up on it.

—WENDELL BERRY

Observe the light of the divine presence that pervades all existence. Observe the harmony of the heavenly realm, how it pervades every aspect of life, the spiritual and the material, which are before your eyes of flesh and your eyes of the spirit.   —ABRAHAM ISAAC KOOK

This is my Father's world.
O let me ne'er forget
that though the wrong seems oft so strong,
God is the ruler yet.   —MALTBIE D. BABCOCK

There's nothing harder to stop than somebody who wants to believe a miracle.   —LESLIE FORD

God speaks to us in a thousand voices, each with the same message: "I love you. Please trust me on this one."
—HUGH PRATHER

CREDITS

Introduction

John Lennon, "Beautiful Boy (Darling Boy)," from the CD *Double Fantasy*, produced by John Lennon, Yoko Ono, and Jack Douglas. Copyright © Capitol Records, 2000.

Rabbi Simeon ben Zoma, chapter 4, Mishna 1(a), quoted in *The Pirkei Avos Treasury: Ethics of the Fathers* (Brooklyn, N.Y.: Menorah Publications, 2003).

Part 1: Find Your Place

Percy C. Ainsworth, *A Little Anthology*, arr. Leslie F. Church (London: Epworth Press, 1939), 37.

Augustine of Hippo: Selected Writings, trans. Mary T. Clark (Ramsey, N.J.: Paulist Press, 1984), 122.

Robert Benson, *Between the Dreaming and the Coming True: The Road Home to God* (San Francisco: HarperSanFrancisco, 1996), 68.

Wendell Berry, *What Are People For?* (New York: North Point Press, 1990), 9.

Jean M. Blomquist, *Wrestling till Dawn: Awakening to Life in Times of Struggle* (Nashville, Tenn.: Upper Room Books, 1994), 111.

Dietrich Bonhoeffer, *Meditating on the Word*, ed. and trans. David McI. Gracie (Nashville, Tenn.: Upper Room, 1986), 37.

Martin Buber, *Tales of the Hasidim: The Early Masters*, trans. Olga Marx (New York: Schocken Books, 1975), 251.

Catherine of Siena, *A Life of Total Prayer: Selected Writings of Catherine of Siena*, ed. Keith Beasley-Topliffe (Nashville, Tenn.: Upper Room Books, 2000), 16.

Anton Chekhov, cited in dailydig.bruderhof.org.

Gregory S. Clapper, *Living Your Heart's Desire: God's Call and Your Vocation* (Nashville, Tenn.: Upper Room Books, 2005), 21, 43–44, 97–98.

Dorothy Day, in Jim Forest, "Opening Heart and Home," *Sojourners* (July 2004): 37.

Christopher de Vinck, in Christopher de Vinck and Elizabeth M. Mosbo VerHage, *Compelled to Write to You: Letters on Faith, Love, Service, and Life* (Nashville, Tenn.: Upper Room Books, 2001), 64.

Meister Eckhardt, in J. Heinrich Arnold, *Freedom from Sinful Thoughts* (Farmington, Pa.: Bruderhof Foundation, 2002), 66.

Albert Einstein, *Out of My Later Years*, chap. 51 (1950), in *The Columbia World of Quotations 1996*, bartleby.com.

Mary Engelbreit, in "About Mary," maryengelbreit.com.

Emmet Fox, *Power through Constructive Thinking* (San Francisco: HarperSanFrancisco, 1989), 164–65.

Viktor E. Frankl, *Man's Search for Meaning* (New York: Simon and Schuster, 1963), 157.

André Gide, cited in quotationspage.com.

Elizabeth Goudge, *Green Dolphin Street* (Cutchogue, N.Y.: Buccaneer Books, 2000).

Grif, in *Red vs. Blue: The Blood Gulch Chronicles* (video, 2003), directed by Burnie Burns and Matt Hullum.

Joyce Hollyday, *Then Shall Your Light Rise: Spiritual Formation and Social Witness* (Nashville, Tenn.: Upper Room Books, 1997), 106.

John Irving, *A Prayer for Owen Meany* (New York: Ballantine Books, 1990), 502.

159

Danny Kaye, cited in *The Change-Your-Life Quote Book*, comp. Allen Klein (New York: Gramercy Books, 2000), 87.

Martin Luther King Jr., "The Drum Major Instinct," in *A Testament of Hope: The Essential Writings and Speeches of Martin Luther King, Jr.*, ed. James Melvin Washington (San Francisco: HarperSanFrancisco, 1991), 265.

Christine Lahti, cited in *The Book of Positive Quotations*, comp. John Cook (New York: Gramercy Books, 1999), 76.

William Law, *A Serious Call to a Devout and Holy Life*, in *Total Devotion to God: Selected Writings of William Law*, ed. Keith Beasley-Topliffe (Nashville, Tenn.: Upper Room Books, 2000), 53, 33, 62.

Madeleine L'Engle with Carole F. Chase, *Glimpses of Grace: Daily Thoughts and Reflections* (San Francisco: HarperSanFrancisco, 1996), 16.

Eric Liddell, in *Chariots of Fire* (film, 1981), directed by Hugh Hudson, produced by David Puttnam. Copyright © 1981 Warner Studios.

Thomas Merton, *Thoughts in Solitude* (New York: Farrar, Straus and Giroux, 1958), 47.

Henry Miller, cited in "Sunbeams," *The Sun* (April 2003): 48.

Moby, in Paul Raushenbush, "A Talk with Moby," beliefnet.com.

Myles Munroe, *In Pursuit of Purpose* (Shippensburg, Pa.: Destiny Image, 1992), 46.

Henri J. M. Nouwen, *Here and Now: Living in the Spirit* (New York: Crossroad Publishing Company, 1994), 53.

Parker J. Palmer, *Let Your Life Speak: Listening for the Voice of Vocation* (San Francisco: Jossey-Bass, 2000), 4, 12.

Boris Pasternak, *Doctor Zhivago* (New York: Alfred A. Knopf, 1991), 314.

Robert M. Pirsig, *Zen and the Art of Motorcycle Maintenance: An Inquiry into Values* (New York: William Morrow Quill, 1979), 192–93.

Hugh Prather, *Spiritual Notes to Myself: Essential Wisdom for the 21st Century* (Berkely, Calif.: Conari Press, 1998), xi.

Rainer Maria Rilke, *Letters to a Young Poet*, trans. Joan M. Burnham (Novato, Calif.: New World Library, 2000), 35.

Will Rogers, cited in *Michael Moncur's (Cynical) Quotations*, quotationspage.com.

Oscar Romero, *The Violence of Love: The Pastoral Wisdom of Archbishop Oscar Romero*, comp. & trans. James R. Brockman (San Francisco: Harper & Row, 1988), 136.

Marsha Sinetar, *Do What You Love, the Money Will Follow: Discovering Your Right Livelihood* (New York: Dell Publishing, 1989).

Dorothee Soelle, *The Silent Cry: Mysticism and Resistance* (Minneapolis, Minn.: Fortress Press, 2001), 5.

Douglas V. Steere, "A Biographical Memoir" in Thomas R. Kelly, *A Testament of Devotion* (New York: Harper & Brothers, 1941), 1.

Mother Teresa of Calcutta, *My Life for the Poor*, ed. José Luis Gonzáles-Balado and Janet N. Playfoot (San Francisco: Harper & Row, 1985), 32.

Mother Teresa, cited in "Sunbeams," *The Sun* (February 2002): 48.

Teresa of Avila, *The Way of Perfection*, trans. and ed. E. Allison Peers (New York: Image Books, 1991), 124.

Thomas à Kempis, *The Imitation of Christ*, in *A Pattern for Life: Selected Writings of Thomas à Kempis*, ed. Keith Beasley-Topliffe (Nashville, Tenn.: Upper Room Books, 1998), 13.

Thomas à Kempis, *The Imitation of Christ: A Timeless Classic for Contemporary Readers*, trans.

credits

William C. Creasy (Notre Dame, Ind.: Ave Maria Press, 1989), 39.

Marjorie J. Thompson, *Companions in Christ: The Way of Forgiveness, Participant's Book* (Nashville, Tenn.: Upper Room Books, 2002), 18.

Howard Thurman, in "Perspectives on Zeal," *Spirituality & Health*, spiritualityhealth.com.

Mark Twain, cited in *The Guinness Book of Poisonous Quotes*, comp. Colin Jarman (Chicago: Contemporary Books, 1993), 325.

Brenda Ueland, *If You Want to Write*, 2nd ed. (St. Paul, Minn.: Graywolf Press, 1997), 177–78.

Jim Wallis, "Building Global Justice: We Are the Ones We Have Been Waiting For," Stanford Baccalaureate Address, June 12, 2004.

Wendy M. Wright, *The Vigil: Keeping Watch in the Season of Christ's Coming* (Nashville, Tenn.: Upper Room Books, 1992), 23, 15.

Flora Slosson Wuellner, *Prayer, Fear, and Our Powers: Finding Our Healing, Release, and Growth in Christ* (Nashville, Tenn.: Upper Room Books, 1989), 40.

Olive Wyon, *Prayer* (London: Fontana Books, 1962), 135–36.

Alexander Yelchaninov, in Bert Ghezzi, *Voices of the Saints: A Year of Readings* (New York: Doubleday, 2000), 143.

Part 2: Connect with the Source

J. Heinrich Arnold, *Freedom from Sinful Thoughts* (Farmington, Pa.: Plough Publishing House, 1997), 94.

Augustine, *The Confessions*, trans. Maria Boulding (Hyde Park, N.Y.: New City Press, 1997), 377.

Augustine, *Confessions*, in *Hungering for God: Selected Writings of Augustine*, ed. Keith Beasley-

Topliffe (Nashville, Tenn.: Upper Room Books, 1997), 12, 55.

Bartleby, in *Dogma* (film, 1999), directed by Kevin Smith, produced by Scott Mojer. © 1999 Columbia Tri-Star.

Bernard of Clairvaux, in Ghezzi, *Voices of the Saints*, 87.

Dietrich Bonhoeffer, *Meditating on the Word*, ed. and trans. David McI. Gracie (Nashville, Tenn.: Upper Room, 1986), 37.

Maria Boulding, *Prayer: Our Journey Home* (Ann Arbor, Mich.: Servant Books, 1980), 11.

Brigitta of Sweden, *Life and Selected Revelations* (New York: Paulist Press, 1990), 214.

Heywood Broun, cited in quotationspage.com.

Lenny Bruce, cited in *The Guinness Book of Poisonous Quotes*, comp. Jarman, 222.

Archie Bunker, *All in the Family* (television show, 1971), directed by Paul Bogart and Norman Campbell, produced by Norman Lear.

Luis Buñuel, cited in *The Guinness Book of Poisonous Quotes*, comp. Jarman, 222.

Carlo Carretto, *The God Who Comes*, trans. Rose Mary Hancock (Maryknoll, N.Y.: Orbis Books, 1974), 3.

Carlo Carretto, *I Sought and I Found: My Experience of God and of the Church*, trans. Robert Barr (Maryknoll, N.Y.: Orbis Books, 1984), 18.

Gregory S. Clapper, *As If the Heart Mattered: A Wesleyan Spirituality* (Nashville, Tenn.: Upper Room Books, 1997), 58.

John Climacus, *The Ladder of Divine Ascent*, trans. Colm Luibheid and Norman Russell (New York: Paulist Press, 1982), 277.

Colette, in Ghezzi, *Voices of the Saints*, 148.

Alice Cooper, in Doug Van Pelt, *Rock Stars on God: 20 Artists Speak Their Minds about Faith* (Lake Mary, Fla.: Relevant Books, 2004), 158.

Dorothy Day, *The Long Loneliness: The Autobiography of Dorothy Day* (San Francisco: HarperSanFrancisco, 1981), 12.

Charles de Foucauld, *Meditations of a Hermit,* trans. Charlotte Balfour (London: Burns & Oates, 1981), 17.

Francis de Sales, *Introduction to the Devout Life,* trans. John K. Ryan (New York: Image Books, 2003), 269.

Esther de Waal, *Living with Contradiction: Reflections on the Rule of St. Benedict* (San Francisco: Harper & Row, 1989), 54.

Ron DelBene with Herb and Mary Montgomery, *Alone with God: A Guide for Personal Retreats,* rev. ed. (Nashville, Tenn.: Upper Room Books, 1992), 126.

Michael J. "Crocodile" Dundee, in *Crocodile Dundee* (film, 1986), directed by Peter Faiman, produced by John Cornell. © 1986 Paramount Studio.

Eddie, in *Keen Eddie* (television show, 2003), created by J. H. Wyman, produced by Warren Littlefield, J. H. Wyman and Simon West.

Albert Einstein, cited in *The Book of Positive Quotations,* comp. Cook, 115.

Thomas C. Ettinger and Helen R. Neinast, *God Goes to College: Living Faith on Campus* (Nashville, Tenn.: Upper Room Books, 2003), 43–44.

Edward Farrell, *Prayer Is a Hunger* (Denville, N.J.: Dimension Books, 1972), 23.

James C. Fenhagen, *Invitation to Holiness* (San Francisco: HarperSanFrancisco, 1985), 31.

Kathleen Fischer, *Winter Grace: Spirituality and Aging* (Nashville, Tenn.: Upper Room Books, 1998), 33.

Harry Emerson Fosdick, cited in *The Book of Positive Quotations,* comp. Cook, 152.

God, in *Joan of Arcadia* (television show, 2003).

Thomas H. Green, *When the Well Runs Dry* (Notre Dame, Ind.: Ave Maria Press, 1979), 54–55.

Stewie Griffin, *Family Guy* (television show, 1999).

Hildegard of Bingen, *Scivias* (1150), in *Meditations with Hildegard of Bingen,* ed. Gabriele Uhlein (Rochester, Vt.: Bear & Company, 1983).

John of the Cross, *The Ascent of Mount Carmel,* in *The Collected Works of St. John of the Cross,* trans. Kieran Kavanaugh and Otilio Rodriguez (Washington, D.C.: ICS Publications, 1979), 102.

Julian of Norwich, *Revelations of Divine Love,* trans. Elizabeth Spearing (London: Penguin Books, 1999).

Toyohiko Kagawa, *Love, the Law of Life* (St. Paul, Minn.: Macalester Park Publishing, 1951), 27.

Thomas R. Kelly, *A Testament of Devotion* (San Francisco: HarperSanFrancisco, 1996), 9.

Thomas R. Kelly, *The Eternal Promise* (London: Hodder and Stoughton, 1966), 103.

Law, *A Serious Call to a Devout and Holy Life,* in *Total Devotion to God: Selected Writings of William Law,* ed. Beasley-Topliffe, 32.

C. S. Lewis, *Mere Christianity,* rev. ed. (New York: Collier Books, 1952), 174.

Eileen Lyddon, *Door through Darkness: John of the Cross and Mysticism in Everyday Life* (Hyde Park, N.Y.: New City Press, 1995), 26.

George A. Maloney, *Bright Darkness: Jesus—Lover of Mankind* (Denville, N.J.: Dimension Books, 1977), 103, 42.

Kyle Matthews, "See for Yourself," in "Journal," kylematthews.com.

credits

Gerald G. May, *The Dark Night of the Soul: A Psychiatrist Explores the Connection between Darkness and Spiritual Growth* (San Francisco: HarperSanFrancisco, 2004), 47.

Thomas Merton, *New Seeds of Contemplation* (New York: New Directions, 1972), 224.

Metatron, in *Dogma* (film, 1999), directed by Kevin Smith, produced by Scott Mojer. © 1999 Columbia Tri-Star.

Calvin Miller, *Leadership* (Colorado Springs, Colo.: NavPress, 1987), 33.

Nancy Mitford, *Pigeon Pie* (New York: Carroll & Graf Publishers, 1987).

Susan Muto, *Womanspirit: Reclaiming the Deep Feminine in Our Human Spirituality* (New York: Crossroad Publishing Company, 1991), 62.

John Henry Newman, *Meditations and Devotions* (London: Longmans, Green and Company, 1953), 277.

Tsar Nicholas II, in *Rasputin* (film, 1996), directed by Uli Edel. © 1996 HBO Studios.

John O'Donohue, *Eternal Echoes: Exploring Our Yearning to Belong* (New York: HarperCollins, 1999), 165.

J. B. Phillips, *Your God Is Too Small* (New York: Touchstone, 1997), 121.

Richard Rohr, *Everything Belongs: The Gift of Contemplative Prayer*, rev. ed. (New York: Crossroad Publishing Company, 2003), 24.

Romero, *The Violence of Love*, comp. and trans. Brockman, 222.

W. E. Sangster, *Teach Me to Pray* (Nashville, Tenn.: Upper Room Books, 1999), 75.

Dana Scully, in *The X Files* (television show, 1993). © 1993 Twentieth Century Fox Home Video.

Shalika, in *Boyz N the Hood* (film, 1991), directed by John Singleton, produced by Steve Nicolaides. © 1991 Columbia/TriStar Studios.

Margaret Silf, *Lighted Windows: Advent Reflections for a World in Waiting* (Nashville, Tenn.: Upper Room Books, 2004), 97.

N. Graham Standish, *Forming Faith in a Hurricane: A Spiritual Primer for Daily Living* (Nashville, Tenn.: Upper Room Books, 1998), 67.

Harriet Beecher Stowe, *The Pearl of Orr's Island: A Story of the Coast of Maine* (Boston: Houghton Mifflin, 2001), 326.

Thomas à Kempis, *The Imitation of Christ*, trans. William C. Creasy (Notre Dame, Ind.: Ave Maria Press, 1989), 71, 77.

Sheldon Vanauken, cited in Kathryn Lindskoog, "Sheldon Vanauken," *The Lewis Legacy* (Winter 1997), discovery.org.

Weil, *Waiting for God*, trans. Craufurd, 133.

John Wesley, *The Works of John Wesley, vol. 18, Journal and Diaries I*, ed. W. Reginald Ward and Richard P. Heitzenrater (Nashville, Tenn.: Abingdon Press, 1988), 249–50.

John Wesley, *A Plain Account of Christian Perfection* (London: Epworth Press, 1952), 101, 102.

John Greenleaf Whittier, "The Eternal Goodness" in *The Poetical Works of John Greenleaf Whittier* (Edinburgh: W. P. Nimmo, Hay, & Mitchell, n.d.), 380.

Oscar Wilde, cited in quotationspage.com.

Wendy M. Wright, *The Time Between: Cycles and Rhythms in Ordinary Time* (Nashville, Tenn.: Upper Room Books), 122.

Flora Slosson Wuellner, *Release: Healing from Wounds of Family, Church, and Community* (Nashville, Tenn.: Upper Room Books, 1996), 63.

credits

Part 3: Belong to a Village

Shirley Abbott, *Womenfolks: Growing Up Down South* (New Haven, Conn.: Tichnor & Fields, 1983).

Percy C. Ainsworth, *A Little Anthology,* arr. Leslie F. Church, 60–61.

Shana Alexander, *Talking Woman* (New York: Delacorte Press, 1976), 177.

Eberhard Arnold, *Salt and Light: Living the Sermon on the Mount* (Farmington, Pa.: Plough Publishing House, 1998), 13.

Augustine, *Confessions,* and "On the Lord's Prayer," sermon LVI, in *Hungering for God: Selected Writings of Augustine,* ed. Keith Beasley-Topliffe (Nashville, Tenn.: Upper Room Books, 1997), 27, 75.

Wendell Berry, *Life Is a Miracle: An Essay against Modern Superstition* (Washington, D.C.: Counterpoint, 2000), 150.

Dietrich Bonhoeffer, *Life Together,* trans. John W. Doberstein (New York: Harper & Row, 1954), 97–98, 78, 20, 19, 26.

Edna Buchanan, *Suitable for Framing* (New York: Warner Books, 1996).

Frederick Buechner, *The Hungering Dark* (New York: Seabury Press, 1969), 87.

George Carlin, cited in "Sunbeams," *The Sun* (April 2004), 48.

Catherine of Siena, *The Letters of Catherine of Siena, vol. 1,* in *A Life of Total Prayer: Selected Writings of Catherine of Siena,* ed. Keith Beasley-Topliffe (Nashville, Tenn.: Upper Room Books, 2000), 13.

William Sloane Coffin, *Credo* (Louisville, Ky.: Westminster John Knox Press, 2004), 21.

Colette, "The Cat," in *The Collected Stories of Colette,* ed. Robert G. Phelps, trans. Matthew Ward and Antonia White (New York: Farrar, Straus and Giroux, 1984).

Dorothy Day, in *By Little and By Little: The Selected Writings of Dorothy Day,* ed. Robert Ellsberg (New York: Alfred A. Knopf, 1983), 330.

Marlene Dietrich, in *Popcorn in Paradise: The Wit and Wisdom of Hollywood,* comp. John Robert Colombo (Austin, Tex.: Holt, Rinehart and Winston, 1980).

Fyodor Dostoyevsky, *The Brothers Karamazov,* trans. Richard Pevear and Larissa Volokhonsky (New York: Farrar, Straus and Giroux, 1990), 322.

Verna Dozier, *Journal of the Episcopal Diocese of Tennessee* (May–June 1992).

Penny Ford, "When the Ritalin Runs Out: Multi-Media vs. Multi-Sensory in College Worship" (unpublished paper, November 17, 2002), 7.

Shere Hite, *The Hite Report on the Family: Growing Up under Patriarchy* (New York: Grove Press, 1996).

James Houston, *The Transforming Friendship* (Oxford: Lion Publishing, 1989), 283.

Jane Howard, *Families* (New York: Simon & Schuster, 1978).

Timothy Jones, *Finding a Spiritual Friend: How Friends and Mentors Can Make Your Faith Grow* (Nashville, Tenn.: Upper Room Books, 1998), 48, 45.

Søren Kierkegaard, *Provocations: Spiritual Writings of Kierkegaard,* comp. and ed. Charles E. Moore (Farmington, Pa.: Plough Publishing House, 1999), 12.

Frank C. Laubach, *Prayer: The Mightiest Force in the World* (Westwood, N.J.: Fleming H. Revell, 1959), 31.

William Law, *A Serious Call to a Devout and Holy Life,* in *Total Devotion to God: Selected Writings of William Law,* 59.

Harper Lee, *To Kill a Mockingbird* (New York: Warner Books, 1982), 34.

Elizabeth Leseur, in Ghezzi, *Voices of the Saints*, 188.

C. S. Lewis, *The Four Loves* (San Diego: Harcourt Brace & Company, 1991), 121.

Martin Luther, in *Eerdmans' Book of Famous Prayers*, comp. Veronica Zundel (Grand Rapids, Mich.: William B. Eerdmans, 1983), 43.

Shirley MacLaine, *Dancing in the Light* (Toronto: Bantam Books, 1985), 291.

Margaret Mead, speech (1975), cited in Michèle Brown and Ann O'Connor, *Woman Talk: A Woman's Book of Quotes*, vol. 1 (Cheltenham, Great Britain.: MacDonald Young Books, 1984).

A. A. Milne, *The World of Pooh: The Complete Winnie-the-Pooh and The House at Pooh Corner* (New York: E. P. Dutton, 1957), 261.

Helen R. Neinast and Thomas C. Ettinger, *With Heart and Mind and Soul: A Guide to Prayer for College Students and Young Adults* (Nashville, Tenn.: Upper Room Books, 1994), 87.

Henri J. M. Nouwen, *Out of Solitude: Three Meditations on the Christian Life* (Notre Dame, Ind.: Ave Maria Press, 1974), 34.

Marilyn Brown Oden, *Abundance: Joyful Living in Christ* (Nashville, Tenn.: Upper Room Books, 2002), 16.

Ana Maria Pineda, "Hospitality," in *Practicing Our Faith: A Way of Life for a Searching People*, ed. Dorothy C. Bass (San Francisco: Jossey-Bass, 1997), 35.

Hugh Prather, *Spiritual Notes to Myself*, 103.

Joan Puls, *Seek Treasures in Small Fields* (Mystic, Conn.: Twenty-Third Publications, 1994), 9.

Rainer Maria Rilke, *Letters to a Young Poet*, trans. M. D. Herter Norton (New York: W. W. Norton, 1993), 59.

Romero, *The Violence of Love*, comp. and trans. Brockman, 222.

Joyce Rupp, *Inviting God In: Scriptural Reflections and Prayers throughout the Year* (Notre Dame, Ind.: Ave Maria Press, 2001), 42.

May Sarton, *Kinds of Love* (New York: W. W. Norton & Company, 1983).

Teresa of Avila, *The Interior Castle*, trans. E. Allison Peers (New York: Image Books, 1972).

Teresa of Avila, in Timothy Jones, *Finding a Spiritual Friend: How Friends and Mentors Can Make Your Faith Grow* (Nashville, Tenn.: Upper Room Books, 1998), 21.

Mother Teresa, *In My Own Words*, comp. José Luis González-Balado (Liguori, Mo.: Liguori Publications, 1996), 91, 28.

Thérèse of Lisieux, *The Autobiography of St. Thérèse of Lisieux: The Story of a Soul*, trans. John Beevers (Garden City, N.Y.: Image Books, 1957), 156.

Caitlin Thomas, *Not Quite Posthumous Letter to My Daughter* (Boston: Little, Brown & Company, 1963), 35.

Howard Thurman, *Meditations of the Heart* (New York: Harper & Brothers, 1953), 49.

Jean Vanier, *Community and Growth: Our Pilgrimage Together* (New York: Paulist Press, 1979), 7, 4, 6.

Doug Van Pelt, *Rock Stars on God*, 65.

Elizabeth M.Mosbo VerHage, in de Vinck and VerHage, *Compelled to Write to You*, 19.

Shellie R. Warren, *Inside of Me: Lessons of Lust, Love and Redemption* (Lake Mary, Fla.: Relevant Books, 2004), 130–31.

Simone Weil, *Waiting for God,* trans. Craufurd, 115, 97.

John Wesley, *A Plain Account of Christian Perfection,* 90.

Olive Wyon, *Prayer,* 139.

Philip Yancey, *What's So Amazing about Grace?* (Grand Rapids, Mich.: Zondervan, 1997), 71.

Part 4: Do the Right Thing

Percy C. Ainsworth, *A Little Anthology,* arr. Church, 44, 28.

Anthony, *Life of Anthony,* in *Seeking a Purer Christian Life: Sayings and Stories of the Desert Fathers and Mothers,* ed. Keith Beasley-Topliffe (Nashville, Tenn.: Upper Room Books, 2000), 23.

J. Heinrich Arnold, in *Discipleship: Living for Christ in the Daily Grind,* comp. and ed. Bruderhof Communities (Farmington, Pa.: Plough Publishing House, 2004), 83.

King Arthur, in *First Knight* (film, 1995), directed by Jerry Zucker, produced by Hunt Lowry and Jerry Zucker. © 1995 Columbia/TriStar Studios.

Augustine, "Faith, Hope, and Love," in *Hungering for God: Selected Writings of Augustine,* ed. Keith Beasley-Topliffe (Nashville, Tenn.: Upper Room Books, 1997), 81–82.

Amelia E. Barr, *All the Days of My Life* (New York: Arno Press, 1980).

Bono, recounting a pastor's advice to him, in Cathleen Falsani, "Bono's American Prayer," *Christianity Today* 47, no. 3 (March 2003): 38.

Charles Borromeo, in Ghezzi, *Voices of the Saints,* 213.

Frederick Buechner, *Brendan* (San Francisco: Harper & Row, 1988), 217.

Carlo Carretto, *The God Who Comes,* trans. Hancock, 10.

"Desires," in *Carmina Gadelica: Hymns & Incantations Collected in the Highlands and Islands of Scotland in the Last Century,* comp. Alexander Carmichael (Edinburgh: Floris Books, 1994), 48.

William Sloane Coffin, *Credo,* 9.

Alice Cooper, in Van Pelt, *Rock Stars on God,* 163.

Charles Caleb Cotton, cited in *The Guinness Book of Poisonous Quotes,* comp. Jarman , 223.

Agnes de Mille, *Dance to the Piper* (Rochester, Great Britain: Columbus Books Limited, 1987).

Meister Eckhart, *Meister Eckhart: A Modern Translation,* trans. Raymond Bernard Blakney (New York: Harper & Row, 1941), 157.

Marian Wright Edelman, *Families in Peril: An Agenda for Social Change* (Cambridge, Mass.: Harvard University Press, 1989).

George Eliot, *Middlemarch,* ed. Rosemary Ashton (London: Penguin Books, 1994), 733–34.

Thomas C. Ettinger and Helen R. Neinast, *God Goes to College,* 112.

Jeff Goldblum, in *Jurassic Park* (film, 1993), directed by Steven Spielberg. © 1993 Universal Studios.

Sammy Hagar, in Van Pelt, *Rock Stars on God,* 39.

Barbara Grizzuti Harrison, "Moral Ambiguity," *Off Center: Essays* (New York: Dial Press, 1980).

Joan of Arc, in *The Messenger: The Story of Joan of Arc* (film, 1999), directed by Luc Besson, produced by Patrice Ledoux. © 1999 Columbia Tri-Star.

Timothy Jones, *Finding a Spiritual Friend,* 36.

Thomas R. Kelly, *A Testament of Devotion,* 77.

Morton Kelsey, *Set Your Hearts on the Greatest Gift: Living the Art of Christian Love* (Nashville, Tenn.: Upper Room Books, 1996), 62.

credits

William Law, *A Serious Call to a Devout and Holy Life*, in *Total Devotion to God: Selected Writings of William Law*, 33.

Karen Lee-Thorp, *A Compact Guide to the Bible* (Colorado Springs, Colo.: NavPress, 2001), 19.

Madeleine L'Engle, *Walking on Water: Reflections on Faith and Art* (Colorado Springs, Colo.: Shaw Books, 2001).

Abraham Lincoln, cited in Jim Wallis, "Communicating Religiously," *Sojo Mail* (September 15, 2004), www.sojourners.net.

Max Lucado, *In the Grip of Grace* (Dallas, Tex.: Word Publishing, 1996), 83.

Clare Boothe Luce, attributed, in Harold Faber, *The Book of Laws* (New York: Times Books, 1979).

Kyle Matthews, "Unchanged," in "Journal," kylematthews.com.

Tom Morello of Rage Against the Machine, in Van Pelt, *Rock Stars on God*, 8.

Ethel Watts Mumford, in Oliver Herford, Ethel Watts Mumford, and Addison Mizner, *The Complete Cynic* (San Francisco: Paul Elder & Company, 1902).

Helen R. Neinast and Thomas C. Ettinger, *With Heart and Mind and Soul: A Guide to Prayer for College Students and Young Adults* (Nashville, Tenn.: Upper Room Books, 1994), 170.

Henri J. M. Nouwen, *Turn My Mourning into Dancing: Moving through Hard Times with Hope*, ed. Timothy Jones (Nashville, Tenn.: W Publishing Group, 2001), 85.

Parker J. Palmer, *Let Your Life Speak*, 78.

Hugh Prather, *Spiritual Notes to Myself*, 28.

Albert Schweitzer, *Reverence for Life*, trans. Reginald H. Fuller (New York: Harper & Row, 1969), 41.

George Bernard Shaw, cited in *The Guinness Book of Poisonous Quotes*, comp. Jarman, 230.

Jennifer Stone, "Lesbian Liberation," in *Mind over Media: Essays on Movie and Television* (Burien, Wa.: Cayuse Press, 1987).

Thomas à Kempis, *The Imitation of Christ*, trans. Creasy, 30–31.

Thomas à Kempis, *The Imitation of Christ*, in *A Pattern for Life: Selected Writings of Thomas à Kempis*, ed. Beasley-Topliffe, 27, 13.

Harry S. Truman, cited in *The Guinness Book of Poisonous Quotes*, 230.

Evelyn Underhill, *The Spiritual Life: Four Broadcast Talks* (London: Hodder & Stoughton, 1937), 36, 84.

Evelyn Underhill, *Light of Christ* (London: Longmans, Green and Company, 1944), 41–42.

Evelyn Underhill, *The House of the Soul*, in *The Soul's Delight: Selected Writings of Evelyn Underhill*, ed. Keith Beasley-Topliffe (Nashville, Tenn.: Upper Room Books, 1998), 45.

Doug Van Pelt, *Rock Stars on God*, 229.

Jim Wallis, "Building Global Justice," Stanford Baccalaureate Address, June 12, 2004.

Elizabeth M.Mosbo VerHage, in de Vinck and VerHage, *Compelled to Write to You*, 18.

Mae West, cited in *The Guinness Book of Poisonous Quotes*, 337.

Oscar Wilde, *Lady Windermere's Fan* (1892), act 1, cited in May, *The Dark Night of the Soul*, 135.

Ella Winter, *And Not to Yield: An Autobiography* (New York: Harcourt, Brace & World, 1963).

John Woolman, *Walking Humbly with God: Selected Writings of John Woolman*, ed. Keith Beasley-Topliffe (Nashville, Tenn.: Upper Room Books, 2000), 32.

credits

Wendy M. Wright, *The Time Between*, 45.

Olive Wyon, *Prayer*, 131.

David Yount, *What Are We to Do?: Living the Sermon on the Mount* (Franklin, Wis.: Sheed & Ward, 2002), 19.

Part 5: Embrace Your Drama

Percy C. Ainsworth, *A Little Anthology*, arr. Church, 59, 28.

Augustine, *Confessions*, in *Hungering for God: Selected Writings of Augustine*, ed. Beasley-Topliffe, 35.

Georges Bernanos, *The Diary of a Country Priest*, trans. Pamela Morris (New York: Carroll & Graf Publishers, 1983), 103.

Wendell Berry, "Heaven in Henry County," *Sojourners* (July 2004): 16.

Jean M. Blomquist, *Wrestling till Dawn: Awakening to Life in Times of Struggle* (Nashville, Tenn.: Upper Room Books, 1994), 27, 107.

Margueritte Harmon Bro, *Sarah* (Markham, Ontario: Fitzhenry & Whiteside, 2001).

Elizabeth Barrett Browning, *The Complete Works of Elizabeth Barrett Browning*, eds. Charlotte Porter and Helen A. Clarke (New York: Crowell, 1900).

Elizabeth J. Canham, *Heart Whispers: Benedictine Wisdom for Today* (Nashville, Tenn.: Upper Room Books, 1999), 111.

Elizabeth J. Canham, *A Table of Delight: Feasting with God in the Wilderness* (Nashville, Tenn.: Upper Room Books, 2005), 15–16.

John Cassian, *Institutes of the Communities*, in *Making Life a Prayer: Selected Writings of John Cassian*, ed. Keith Beasley-Topliffe (Nashville, Tenn.: Upper Room Books, 1997), 18.

Catherine of Siena, *The Letters of Catherine of Siena*, vol. 1, in *A Life of Total Prayer: Selected Writings of Catherine of Siena*, ed. Beasley-Topliffe, 14.

Gregory S. Clapper, *Living Your Heart's Desire*, 29.

Marilla Cuthbert, in *Anne of Green Gables* (television show, 1985), directed by Kevin Sullivan. © 1986 Uav Corporation.

Charles de Foucauld, *Meditations of a Hermit*, trans. Balfour, 134.

Marian Wright Edelman, *Families in Peril*.

Kathleen Fischer, *Winter Grace: Spirituality and Aging* (Nashville, Tenn.: Upper Room Books, 1998), 8–9.

Francis of Assisi, in Ghezzi, *Voices of the Saints*, 185.

Viktor E. Frankl, *Man's Search for Meaning* (New York: Simon and Schuster, 1963), 104.

Kent Ira Groff, *Journeymen: A Spiritual Guide for Men (and for Women Who Want to Understand Them)* (Nashville, Tenn.: Upper Room Books, 1999), 16.

Etty Hillesum, *An Interrupted Life: The Diaries of Etty Hillesum*, 1941–43, trans. Arno Pomerans (New York: Pantheon Books, 1983), 129.

Joyce Huggett, *Formed by the Desert* (Guildford, England: Eagle, 1997), 60.

John Indermark, *Turn Toward Promise: The Prophets and Spiritual Renewal* (Nashville, Tenn.: Upper Room Books, 2004), 96.

Mary Jean Irion, *Yes, World: A Mosaic of Meditation* (Calgary, Alberta: Cambria Press, 1970).

Rueben P. Job, in Norman Shawchuck and Rueben P. Job, *A Guide to Prayer for All Who Seek God* (Nashville, Tenn. Upper Room Books, 2003), 135.

W. Paul Jones, *A Season in the Desert: Making Time Holy* (Brewster, Mass.: Paraclete Press, 2000), 154.

Julian of Norwich: Showings, trans. Edmund Colledge and James Walsh (New York: Paulist Press, 1978), 165.

Julian of Norwich, *Revelations of Divine Love*, quoted in Rosalie Maggio, *The New Beacon Book of Quotations by Women* (Boston: Beacon Press, 1996), 665.

John Killinger, *Beginning Prayer* (Nashville, Tenn.: Upper Room Books, 1981), 106.

Anne Morrow Lindbergh, *Hour of Gold, Hour of Lead: Diaries and Letters of Anne Morrow Lindbergh, 1929–1932* (New York: Harcourt, 1973).

Brennan Manning, *The Wisdom of Tenderness: What Happens When God's Fierce Mercy Transforms Our Lives* (San Francisco: HarperSanFrancisco, 2002), 152–53.

Catherine Marshall, *Christy* (New York: Avon Books, 1967).

Suzanne Massie, in Robert K. and Suzanne Massie, *Journey* (New York: Alfred A. Knopf, 1975).

Gerald G. May, *The Dark Night of the Soul*, 182.

Paul McCartney, "Let It Be" from the album *Let It Be*. © 1970 Apple/Parlophone PCS 7096.

Henri J. M. Nouwen, *The Inner Voice of Love* (New York: Doubleday, 1996), 109.

Henri J. M. Nouwen, *Turn My Mourning into Dancing*, 11, 51.

Henri J. M. Nouwen, *Here and Now*, 32–33.

Joyce Carol Oates, speech given at Festival of Faith and Writing, Calvin College, Grand Rapids, Mich., April 2004.

Parker J. Palmer, *Let Your Life Speak*, 70.

Porgy, in *Porgy and Bess* (video, 1993), opera created by George Gershwin, video directed by Trevor Nunn. © 2001 EMI Distribution.

Hugh Prather, *Spiritual Notes to Myself*, 3.

Richard Rohr, *Everything Belongs*, rev. ed., 33.

Christina Rossetti, "From House to Home," in *The Complete Poems of Christina Rossetti*, ed. R. W. Crump (Baton Rouge, La.: Louisiana State University Press, 1979), 88.

May Sarton, *Journal of a Solitude* (New York: W. W. Norton & Company, 1973).

Margaret Silf, *Lighted Windows: Advent Reflections for a World in Waiting* (Nashville, Tenn.: Upper Room Books, 2004), 94.

Hannah Whitall Smith, *The Christian's Secret of a Happy Life* (Chicago: Fleming H. Revell, 1888), 240.

Charles H. Spurgeon, *Morning and Evening: Daily Readings* (McLean, Va.: MacDonald Publishing, n.d.), 634.

Lt. Daniel Taylor, in *Forrest Gump* (film, 1994), directed by Robert Zemeckis; produced by Wendy Finerman, Steve Tisch, and Steve Starkey. © 1994 Paramount Studio.

Teresa of Avila, *The Interior Castle*, trans. E. Allison Peers (New York: Image Books, 1989).

Tevye, in *Fiddler on the Roof* (film, 1971), directed and produced by Norman Jewison. © 1971 United Artists.

Thomas à Kempis, *The Imitation of Christ*, in *A Pattern for Life*, ed. Beasley-Topliffe, 30, 16.

Howard Thurman, *The Inward Journey* (Richmond, Ind.: Friends United Press, 1971), 48.

Paul Tillich, *The Shaking of the Foundations* (New York: Charles Scribner's Sons, 1948), 161–62.

Geoff Tipps, *The League of Gentlemen* (television show, 1999), created by Steve Pemberton, Reece Shearsmith, Mark Gatiss, and Jeremy Dyson.

John Wesley, *A Plain Account of Christian Perfection*, in *A Longing for Holiness: Selected Writings of John Wesley*, ed. Keith Beasley-Topliffe (Nashville, Tenn.: Upper Room Books, 1997), 63.

Thornton Wilder, *The Angel That Troubled the Waters, and Other Plays* (New York: Coward-McCann Publishers, 1928), 147 ff.

Olive Wyon, *Prayer*, 117.

Part 6: Go for Broke

Patch Adams, in *Patch Adams* (film, 1998), directed by Tom Shadyac, produced by Barry Kemp, Mike Farrell, Marvin Minoff, and Charles Newirth. © 1998 Universal Studios.

Percy C. Ainsworth, *A Little Anthology*, arr. Church, 21.

Marie Antoinette, on the way to the guillotine (1793), cited in Maggio, *The New Beacon Book of Quotations by Women*, 146.

King Arthur, in *First Knight* (film, 1995), directed by Jerry Zucker, produced by Hunt Lowry, Jerry Zucker. © 1995 Columbia/TriStar Studios.

Jean M. Blomquist, *Wrestling till Dawn*, 67.

Dietrich Bonhoeffer, *The Cost of Discipleship* (New York: Simon & Schuster, 1995), 89.

Fanny Burney, *Evelina: or, The History of a Young Lady's Entrance into the World* (New York: Modern Library, 2001).

Andy, in *The Shawshank Redemption* (film, 1994), cited in Clapper, *Living Your Heart's Desire*, 57.

William Sloane Coffin, *Credo*, 7.

Mary Daly, cited at Re-Imagining Community gathering, Minneapolis, Minn., October 27, 2001.

Geena Davis, in Kevin Sessums, "Geena's Sheen," *Vanity Fair*, 1992.

Christopher de Vinck, in de Vinck and VerHage, *Compelled to Write to You:*, 26, 63.

Annie Dillard, *Pilgrim at Tinker Creek* (New York: HarperPerennial, 1985), 268.

Annie Dillard, *Teaching a Stone to Talk* (New York: Harper & Row, 1988), 40–41.

Maxie Dunnam, *Let Me Say That Again: Maxims for Spiritual Living* (Nashville, Tenn.: Upper Room Books, 1996).

Elizabeth Warnock Fernea, *A View of the Nile* (New York: Doubleday, 1970). |

Kathleen Fischer, *Winter Grace*, 18.

Harry Emerson Fosdick, cited in *The Book of Positive Quotations*, comp. Cook, 302.

Sarah Leah Grafstein, in Sherry Ruth Anderson and Patricia Hopkins, *The Feminine Face of God: The Unfolding of the Sacred in Women* (New York: Bantam Books, 1991).

Thomas H. Green, *When the Well Runs Dry* (Notre Dame, Ind.: Ave Maria Press, 1979), 97.

Germaine Greer, *The Female Eunuch* (New York: Farrar, Straus and Giroux, 1971).

Emilie Griffin, *Clinging: The Experience of Prayer* (San Francisco: Harper & Row, 1984), 2.

Edith Hamilton, *The Greek Way* (New York: W. W. Norton & Company, 1993).

Dag Hammarskjöld, *Markings*, trans. Leif Sjöberg and W. H. Auden (New York: Alfred A. Knopf, 1998), 55, 7.

Etty Hillesum, *An Interrupted Life*, trans. Pomerans, 196.

credits

E. Glenn Hinson, *Spiritual Formation for Christian Leadership* (Nashville, Tenn.: Upper Room Books, 1999), 40.

Elbert Hubbard, cited in *The Guinness Book of Poisonous Quotes*, comp. Jarman, 8.

Ignatius of Antioch, *Roots of Faith* (Grand Rapids, Mich.: William B. Eerdmans, 1997), 25, 27.

India.Arie, foreword to Shellie R. Warren, *Inside of Me: Lessons of Lust, Love, and Redemption* (Lake Mary, Fla.: Relevant Books, 2004), vii.

William James, cited in *The Change-Your-Life Quote Book*, comp. Klein, 7.

Joan of Arc, in *The Messenger: The Story of Joan of Arc* (film, 1999), directed by Luc Besson, produced by Patrice Ledoux. © 1999 Columbia Tri-Star.

Ben Campbell Johnson, *Calming the Restless Spirit: A Journey toward God* (Nashville, Tenn.: Upper Room Books, 1997), 37.

Thomas Keating, *Open Mind, Open Heart* (Amity, N.Y.: Amity House, 1986), 45.

Helen Keller, *Let Us Have Faith* (New York: Doubleday, 1941).

Thomas R. Kelly, *Reality of the Spiritual World*, in *The Sanctuary of the Soul: Selected Writings of Thomas Kelly*, ed. Keith Beasley-Topliffe (Nashville, Tenn.: Upper Room Books, 1997), 43.

Sue Monk Kidd, *When the Heart Waits* (San Francisco: Harper & Row, 1990), 152.

Harper Lee, *To Kill a Mockingbird* (New York: Warner Books, 1982), 116.

Madeleine L'Engle, *Walking on Water: Reflections on Faith and Art* (Wheaton, Ill.: Harold Shaw Publishers, 1998), 67.

Anne Morrow Lindbergh, *The Wave of the Future: A Confession of Faith* (New York: Harcourt, Brace & World Company, 1940).

Katherine Mansfield, *The Journal of Katherine Mansfield* (Whitefish, Mont.: Kessinger Publishing, 2003).

Kyle Matthews, "My Heart Knows," in "Journal," kylematthews.com.

Gerald May, *The Dark Night of the Soul*, 70.

Phyllis McGinley, in Ghezzi, *Voices of the Saints*, 137.

Alanis Morissette, "Hand in My Pocket," from the album *Jagged Little Pill*. © 1995 Maverick Records.

Rebbe Nachman of Breslov, *The Empty Chair: Finding Hope and Joy*, adap. Moshe Mykoff (Woodstock, Vt.: Jewish Lights Publishing, 1994), 15.

Anaïs Nin, *The Diary of Anaïs Nin*, vol. 3, 1939–1944 (San Diego: Harvest/Harcourt Brace & Company, 1971).

William O. Paulsell, *Taste and See* (Nashville, Tenn.: The Upper Room, 1976), 57.

Eugene H. Peterson, *Working the Angles: The Shape of Pastoral Integrity* (Grand Rapids, Mich.: William B. Eerdmans, 1987), 43–44.

Robert M. Pirsig, *Zen and the Art of Motorcycle Maintenance*, 297.

Miriam Pollard, *The Listening God* (Wilmington, Del.: Michael Glazier, 1989), 93.

Hugh Prather, *Spiritual Notes to Myself*, 116.

Richard Rohr, *Everything Belongs*, 23.

J. D. Salinger, *Franny and Zooey* (Boston: Little, Brown and Company, 1991), 30.

Hannah Whitall Smith, *The Christian's Secret of a Happy Life*, 34.

Julia Sorel, *See How She Runs* (New York: Ballantine Books, 1978).

N. Graham Standish, *Forming Faith in a Hurricane*, 29.

Teresa of Avila, *The Life of Saint Teresa of Avila*, trans. J. M. Cohen (New York: Penguin Books, 1957), 148–49.

Thomas à Kempis, *The Imitation of Christ*, in *A Pattern for Life: Selected Writings of Thomas à Kempis*, ed. Beasley-Topliffe, 26, 25.

Evelyn Underhill, *The House of the Soul*, in *The Soul's Delight: Selected Writings of Evelyn Underhill*, ed. Keith Beasley-Topliffe (Nashville, Tenn.: Upper Room Books, 1998), 30.

Mary Anna Vidakovich, *Meeting God on the Mountain* (Nashville, Tenn.: Upper Room Books, 1996), 94.

Virgil (quoted by Justice Oliver Wendell Holmes on his ninetieth birthday), cited in *The Harper Book of Quotations*, 3rd ed., ed. Robert I. Fitzhenry (New York: HarperPerennial, 1993), 122.

Jim Wallis, "Building Global Justice," Stanford Baccalaureate Address, June 12, 2004.

Simone Weil, *Waiting for God*, trans. Craufurd, 97.

Simone Weil, *Selected Essays, 1934–1943*, trans. Richard Rees (London: Oxford University Press, 1962).

Mae West, in *Klondike Annie* (film, 1936), directed by Raoul Walsh. Video © 1993 Universal Studios.

Morris West, *Three Complete Novels: The Shoes of the Fisherman, The Clowns of God, Lazarus* (New York: Wings Books, 1993), 144.

Agnes Whistling Elk, in Lynn V. Andrews, *Crystal Woman: The Sisters of the Dreamtime* (New York: Warner Books, 1988).

Dallas Willard, *Renovation of the Heart: Putting on the Character of Christ* (Colorado Springs, Colo.: NavPress, 2002), 15.

Flora Slosson Wuellner, *Prayer, Stress, and Our Inner Wounds* (Nashville, Tenn.: Upper Room Books, 1985), 94.

Philip Yancey, *What's So Amazing about Grace?* (Grand Rapids, Mich.: Zondervan Publishing House, 1997), 180.

Part 7: See the Unseen

David Adam, *Forward to Freedom: From Exodus to Easter* (Nashville, Tenn.: Upper Room Books, 2001), 31.

Percy C. Ainsworth, *A Little Anthology*, arr. Church, 27, 37, 22, 33.

Angela, *The Book of Divine Consolation of the Blessed Angela of Foligno* (New York: Duffield & Company, 1909).

Anonymous, cited in *The Guinness Book of Poisonous Quotes*, comp. Jarman, 84.

Augustine, in Evelyn Underhill, *The Ways of the Spirit*, ed. Grace Adolphsen Brame (New York: Crossroad Publishing Company, 1990), 181.

Maltbie D. Babcock, excerpt from "This Is My Father's World," in *The United Methodist Hymnal* (Nashville, Tenn.: The United Methodist Publishing House, 1989), no. 144.

Sue Bender, *Plain and Simple* (San Francisco: HarperSanFrancisco, 1989), 149.

Sue Bender, *Everyday Sacred: A Woman's Journey Home* (San Francisco: HarperSanFrancisco, 1995), 159.

Wendell Berry, *Life Is a Miracle: An Essay against Modern Superstition* (Washington, D.C.: Counterpoint, 2000), 10.

Roberta C. Bondi, *In Ordinary Time: Healing the Wounds of the Heart* (Nashville, Tenn.: Abingdon Press, 1996), 202–03.

credits

Dietrich Bonhoeffer, *Meditating on the Word,* ed. & trans. David McI. Gracie (Nashville, Tenn.: Upper Room, 1986), 44.

The Book of Common Prayer (New York: Oxford University Press, 1990), 827.

Michael Bouttier, *Prayers for My Village* (Nashville, Tenn.: Upper Room Books, 1994), 25.

Elizabeth Barrett Browning, *Aurora Leigh* (Oxford: Oxford University Press, 1993).

Frederick Buechner, *Now and Then* (San Francisco: Harper & Row, 1983), 87.

Elizabeth J. Canham, *Heart Whispers: Benedictine Wisdom for Today* (Nashville, Tenn.: Upper Room Books, 1999), 25.

Ernesto Cardenal, *Abide in Love* (Maryknoll, N.Y.: Orbis Books, 1995), 119.

Thomas Carlyle, cited in *The Guinness Book of Poisonous Quotes,* comp. Jarman, 223.

Catherine of Siena, in Dorothy Day, *By Little and by Little.*

Oswald Chambers, *My Utmost for His Highest* (London: Simpkin Marshall, 1937), 38, 41.

The Cloud of Unknowing, ed. James Walsh (Ramsey, N.J.: Paulist Press, 1981), 265.

Alice Cooper, in Van Pelt, *Rock Stars on God,* 169.

Margaret Deland, *John Ward, Preacher* (New York: Irvington Publishers, 1984).

Christopher de Vinck, in de Vinck and VerHage, *Compelled to Write to You,* 60.

Esther de Waal, *Living with Contradiction: Reflections on the Rule of St. Benedict* (San Francisco: Harper & Row, 1989), 81.

Louis Evely, *Our Prayer* (New York: Herder and Herder, 1970), 65.

Leslie Ford, *Washington Whispers Murder* (New York: Charles Scribner's Sons, 1953).

Harry Emerson Fosdick, in "October 5, 1930: Harry Emerson Fosdick Dedicated Riverside Church," *Christian History Institute,* gospelcom.net.

Bert Ghezzi, *Voices of the Saints,* 13.

Ken Gire, *Windows of the Soul* (Grand Rapids, Mich.: Zondervan Publishing House, 1996), 211.

Thomas H. Green, *When the Well Runs Dry: Prayer Beyond the Beginnings* (Notre Dame, Ind.: Ave Maria Press, 1998), 148.

Thomas H. Green, foreword to Leonard Boase, *The Prayer of Faith* (Chicago: Loyola University Press, 1985), v.

Madame Guyon, *A Short and Easy Method of Prayer* (London: H. R. Allenson, n.d.), 13.

Dag Hammarskjöld, *Markings,* trans. Sjöberg and Auden, 56, 89.

James C. Howell, *Servants, Misfits, and Martyrs,* 17, 31.

John Indermark, *Setting the Christmas Stage,* 33.

Irenaeus, Bishop of Lyons (2nd century CE), *Against Heresies* 4.20.7, www.ccel.org.

Thomas R. Kelly, *A Testament of Devotion,* 100.

John Killinger, *Bread for the Wilderness, Wine for the Journey* (Waco, Tex.: Word Books, 1976), 31.

Abraham Isaac Kook, *Lights of Holiness* (New York: Paulist Press, 1978), 207.

Lawrence Kushner, *Honey from the Rock: Visions of Jewish Mystical Renewal* (Woodstock, Vt.: Jewish Lights Publishing, 1994), 48.

William Law, *A Serious Call to a Devout and Holy Life,* in *Total Devotion to God,* 64.

William Law, *The Spirit of Prayer* (London: Griffith Farran & Co., n.d.), 8.

credits

C. S. Lewis, *Mere Christianity*, 190.

Madeleine L'Engle, *Walking on Water*, 72.

Kyle Matthews, "My Heart Knows," in "Journal," kylematthews.com.

Kyle Matthews, "Sometimes I Picture God That Way," in "Journal," kylematthews.com.

John Maurer, in Van Pelt, *Rock Stars on God*, 80.

Thomas Merton, *Conjectures of a Guilty Bystander* (New York: Image Books, 1989), 157.

Wendy Miller, *Learning to Listen: A Guide for Spiritual Friends* (Nashville, Tenn.: Upper Room Books, 1993), 22.

Robert F. Morneau, *From Resurrection to Pentecost: Easter-Season Meditations* (New York: Crossroad Publishing Company, 2000), 105.

Tsar Nicholas II, in *Nicholas and Alexandra* (film, 1971), directed by Franklin J. Schaffner. Video © 1992 Columbia/TriStar Studios.

Mary Catherine Nolan, *Mary's Song: Living Her Timeless Prayer* (Notre Dame, Ind.: Ave Maria Press, 2001), 24.

Henri J. M. Nouwen, *Turn My Mourning into Dancing*, 60.

Henri J. M. Nouwen, *Bread for the Journey: A Daybook of Wisdom and Faith* (San Francisco: HarperSanFrancisco, 1997), January 1.

Henri J. M. Nouwen, *Finding My Way Home: Pathways to Life and the Spirit* (New York: Crossroad Publishing Company, 2001), 26.

Henri J. M. Nouwen, *Life of the Beloved: Spiritual Living in a Secular World* (New York: Crossroad Publishing Company, 1992), 39.

Delmar O'Donnell, in *O Brother, Where Art Thou?* (film, 2000), directed by Ethan Coen and Joel Coen, produced by Ethan Coen. © 2000 Touchstone.

Isaac Penington, "The Letters of Isaac Penington," in *Quaker Spirituality: Selected Writings*, ed. Douglas V. Steere (New York: Paulist Press, 1984), 143.

Hugh Prather, *Spiritual Notes to Myself*, 7.

Jan L. Richardson, "A Prayer for the Beginning of Lent," in *Sacred Journeys: A Woman's Book of Daily Prayer* (Nashville, Tenn.: Upper Room Books, 1995), 135.

Richard Rohr, *Everything Belongs*, rev. ed., 112, 20.

Albert Schweitzer, *Reverence for Life*, trans. Reginald H. Fuller (New York: Harper & Row, 1969), 93.

Sundar Singh, *With and Without Christ* (New York: Harper & Brothers, 1929), 136—37.

Charles H. Spurgeon, *Morning and Evening*, 626.

Anne-Sophie Swetchine, *The Writings of Madame Swetchine*, ed. Count de Falloux (New York: Catholic Publishing Society, 1869).

Mother Teresa, *In My Own Words*, comp. González-Balado, 7.

Evelyn Underhill, "Thrushes," in *Theophanies: A Book of Verses* (New York: E. P. Dutton, 1916), 94.

Friedrich von Hügel, *The Life of Prayer* (London: J. M. Dent & Sons, 1927), 8.

Alice Walker, *The Color Purple* (New York: Harvest/ Harcourt Brace Jovanovich, 2003).

Kallistos Ware, *The Orthodox Way* (Crestwood, N.Y.: St. Vladimir's Seminary Press, 1980), 23.

Macrina Wiederkehr, in Heather Webb, "Many Come in Darkness: A Conversation with Macrina Wiederkehr," *Mars Hill Review* 9, no. 9 (fall 1997): 79.

Marjorie Wilkinson, *The Good Tree* (Toronto: Ryerson, 1959), 47.

credits

Oprah Winfrey, cited in *The Book of Positive Quotations,* comp. Cook, 249.

David Yount, *What Are We to Do?: Living the Sermon on the Mount* (Franklin, Wis.: Sheed & Ward, 2002), 89.

Don't miss these Upper Room books

Creating a Life with God

The Call of Ancient Prayer Practices

by Daniel Wolpert

This book offers the opportunity to learn and adopt 12 prayer practices. Practices include the general practice of peace and quiet, *lectio divina,* the Jesus Prayer, creativity, journaling, and more. Especially helpful for young adults!

ISBN 0-8358-9855
paperback • 192 pages

To Walk in Integrity

Spiritual Leadership in Times of Crisis

by Steve Doughty

A timely resource for the 21st century! Exploring the biblical understanding of integrity, Doughty identifies 9 key elements in the life of integrity. In this book he tells powerful stories of persons who acted with integrity in difficult situations despite great personal cost. Each chapter includes guidance for personal meditation and group reflection.

ISBN 0-8358-9885-7
paperback • 144 pages

175

Other Offerings from Upper Room Ministries

• Web site for young adults: **www.Methodx.net**—Filled with humor, prayer methods, scripture, and more, MethodX addresses from a Christian perspective the many issues young adults face daily.

• *God Goes to College: Living Faith on Campus* by Thomas C. Ettinger and Helen R. Neinast—In this book for college students, experienced campus ministers Tom Ettinger and Helen Neinast offer perspectives that are both reality-based and Christ-centered. Readers can use this book to nurture their spiritual lives, guide their prayer and reflection, and shape a devotional time for themselves or a group.
ISBN: 0-8358-0987-0 • Paperback • 128 pages

• *Living Your Heart's Desire: God's Call and Your Vocation* by Gregory S. Clapper—This book helps people of any age who are struggling to put their faith and their work together in powerful, meaningful ways.

ISBN 0-8358-9805-9 • Paperback • 128 pages

To order: Visit our Web site, www.upperroom.org, or call 1-800-972-0433.